Instructor's Resource Manual

AMERICAN MOSAIC

Multicultural Readings in Context

Barbara Roche Rico

Loyola Marymount University

Sandra Mano

University of California, Los Angeles

HOUGHTON MIFFLIN COMPANY   BOSTON

Dallas   Geneva, Illinois   Palo Alto   Princeton, New Jersey

CONTENTS

PREFACE

This guide presents suggestions for using AMERICAN MOSAIC effectively.
Because we see both teaching and writing as processes that evolve from the
rhetorical situation and involve the intentions of the teacher and writer, we offer
suggestions rather than rules for procedure. We also have avoided trying to
provide answers to the questions that follow the readings, since we see learning as
a collaborative activity and one that should engage and center on students.
Instead, we encourage you to help students take responsibility of generating their
own questions and answers. To this end, we have included the following features in
our Instructor's Resource Manual:

- An overview of our philosophy of composition
- An outline of the organization of the text
- Suggestions for using the text, including ideas on class organization and
  teaching hints
- Chapter notes that include brief introductions to each reading and classroom
  strategies to enhance individual and collaborative learning
- A thematic table of contents
- Film suggestions

INTRODUCTION

With the increasingly multicultural nature of the United States and the growing number of multicultural and multilingual students in our universities, teachers of composition have become even more aware of the need for readers that present writers who reflect the ethnic diversity of this country. Until recently, such readers have been very scarce. Now a few thematic readers deal with generic themes from a multicultural perspective. Our text presents particularly generative periods in the history of various ethnic groups in the United States and, after setting the context, lets the representative authors speak for themselves about issues of importance to them. We believe that all students will be enriched by sharing the voices of various ethnic writers and by understanding something about the periods in which they wrote and the contributions they made to this country. Students will also develop a fuller appreciation of the multicultural nature of contemporary American society.

This text presents the writing of most ethnic groups in the United States within a chronological framework. Each chapter reflects what we consider a significant period in the development of a particular ethnic group using readings that are representative of the attitudes and concerns of that period. Clearly these people were writing before the period we selected and have continued writing since. Our intention is to suggest the richness of the American experience rather than provide a comprehensive coverage of the American ethnic literature and history.

Organization of AMERICAN MOSAIC

We chose to begin with the 1880s because this period saw a massive influx to the United States of immigrants from Europe and Asia. Chapter 1 presents the writings of some of these immigrants, and serves as a general introduction to the concerns and themes expressed by later immigrants and other ethnic groups in the chapters that follow. Achieving success, coping with discrimination, loss of culture and identity, and generational conflicts appear to be universal concerns.

Chapters 2 through 8 focus on specific ethnic groups. In some chapters, the readings are from a brief and particularly generative period, such as the years of the Japanese internment. In others, such as Chapter 4 on the Puerto Rican writers, they span several years. The difference in focus resulted from several factors, including availability, quality, and relevance of the material.

Chapter 2 focuses on the Chinese immigrants who came to the West Coast in the late 1800s. Chapter 3 turns to the writers of the Harlem Renaissance from the years following World War I to the beginning of the Depression. Chapter 4 surveys the writing of Puerto Ricans in New York, beginning with the 1880s and continuing to the present. Chapter 5 presents the often neglected experience of the Japanese Americans during World War II from their own perspective. Chapter 6 focuses on the civil rights struggle of African Americans for equal opportunity. Chapter 7 introduces the works of Chicano writers. Chapter 8 deals with another renaissance, that of Native American writers.

Chapter 9, like Chapter 1, presents representative voices from several groups. Some speak of the experiences of the many new immigrants to the United States. Others, long-time Americans, reflect on their own personal and cultural histories.

Each chapter begins with an introduction that presents major historical events and conditions of the period that shaped the group or groups represented. This helps students understand the context of the readings. The introduction ends with a section on literary voices that acquaints students with the writers and readings in the chapter. A photo essay at the beginning of each chapter further helps students visualize the historical context. The readings begin with an important historical document that reflects the key issues faced by the group represented. Following that are the selections — short stories, poems, or essays — by authors from the group. Each chapter ends with a contemporary essay that reflects on the issues raised in the chapter from a modern perspective.

Each chapter contains pre-reading, discussion/writing, and connecting questions designed to engage students in the readings, encourage them to read closely, and help them make connections among pieces within chapters and throughout the book.

A Beginning: Pre-reading/Writing activity follows the introduction to the chapter. This exercise aims to get students to think about some aspect of the experiences reported in the chapter before they read the material. This activity generates interest in the topic and encourages students to recall what they already know about the topic; students who are members of the group represented in the chapter can share their expertise. We've designed the pre-reading activity to last approximately one class period. Each pre-reading activity and all of the questions will be discussed in Part 2 of this manual.

Following each selection are three or four Responding questions. Typically one asks students to reread the selection closely. Another often requires a restatement of the author's main points. A third gives students the option to work in small groups. We encourage group work because we believe small-group discussion fosters collaborative learning. Then the teacher and the text are no longer the only sources of knowledge. A fourth question asks for a personal response and aims to help students connect the reading with their own experiences. It is especially important for all students to share experiences when dealing with multicultural readings. Students who are members of the ethnic group being discussed can serve as resources; the remaining students will recognize the common human experience that cuts across ethnic and cultural boundaries.

The Responding questions generally are designed to promote close reading of the text and encourage discussion and writing. Some specifically call for students to discuss or to write, but all can be adapted to either mode. The questions prompt a range of responses from the personal to the scholarly. Most likely you will not want to use all of the questions; rather, you and your students can select whichever questions fit your own interests or classroom situations.

Each chapter ends with an extensive list of Connecting questions. These are designed to promote analytical thinking about the selections and to help students connect ideas, themes, and issues throughout the text. You may find the thematic table of contents in Part Three of this manual helpful in approaching these questions.

The Connecting questions are broader and more complex than the Responding questions that follow each reading. They highlight the similarity of experiences among different ethnic and cultural groups and point up connections to other readings in the text whenever possible. Your students may choose to answer just one question, or individual students may choose different questions and share their answers with the class. We believe students should be given the opportunity to respond to questions that interest them, or to create their own questions. Several of the questions give students the option to design their own essay topic; this approach often engages students more closely and produces livelier essays.

Each set of Connecting questions contains some questions that invite further research. These are intended for classes that include research papers as part of the curriculum. The topics require extensive outside reading.

Before we begin with specifics on how to use this book, we need to say a word about names and naming. One problem in creating a multicultural readings text is the use of names of ethnic groups that may be in the process of changing. We have tried as much as possible to refer to groups by the names they themselves used at particular periods in history. The issue of naming is controversial, however, and would be an interesting topic for class discussion.

PART ONE

SUGGESTIONS FOR USING *AMERICAN MOSAIC*

We have designed this text to be used with process pedagogy. We assume that students will have a voice in deciding on essay topics and that their essays will go through a series of drafts for review by both peers and instructor. We believe the book is adaptable to both a student-centered workshop approach and a traditional classroom setting. Briefly, we want to describe several possible ways of organizing a course using this text. Considerations of time, your own inclinations, and your students' interests and needs will determine which format you choose.

Course Organization

We recommend that you create a writing workshop in your classroom. Such a class focuses on students as readers and writers and aims to transform the classroom into a community of writers. To achieve this end, you will need to involve students in both individual and collaborative activities centered around pre-writing, composing, and editing.

You have several options for organizing your class. Activities can be designed and initiated by you and/or students. Whole-class discussions can be led by you or by individual or groups of students. The important point is to keep the emphasis on reading and writing as a process, that is, on the process used to arrive at the final products rather than on the products themselves. Papers are always in process and are continuously being revised. In such courses, drafts are responded to with comments (oral or written) rather than with grades. Sometimes final drafts are graded throughout the course, but often grading is deferred until a final portfolio of students' best work from the quarter or the semester is compiled at the end of the course. At that time, the papers might be graded by you or by a departmental portfolio system wherein you and your colleagues grade one another's students' papers.

Such a course design allows students to work on individual projects, because the material is not presented in a lecture format. However, there are many ways to organize such a course. You can have students browse through the table of contents in the text and list the chapters that interest them in order of preference. If you choose this method, you can divide the class into groups according to their interests. Each group reads, talks, and writes about material that interests them. Periodically, the groups share their information with the entire class through oral presentations on the readings, sharing of drafts, and so forth. This organization not only allows students to follow their own interests but exposes them to more aspects of the readings than a traditional course could cover. This sharing of students' responses may motivate them to read material other than that assigned. In addition, students usually read and write more effectively when they are personally attracted to the material and have a voice in selecting it.

An alternative method that allows for student choice but keeps the class working together is to have students rank the chapters according to their interests and have the entire class read the chapters in order of class, rather than individual, preference.

Another method of organizing the course is for you to choose the readings. For example, you can assign entire chapters, perhaps one from the beginning, middle, and end of the book; alternatively, you can assign selections from each chapter. We recommend that students read the introductions and the legal documents as well as the final selection in each chapter because these set the historical context for the readings. Then students can read all or some of the selections, depending on your goals and their interests.

At the beginning of the course, you might introduce David Mura's essay in Chapter 9. This reading presents many of the arguments for a course focusing on multicultural issues and writers. Students need not actually read the essay at this time; rather, you can introduce some of the following questions for consideration during the semester or quarter:

1. Who should take ethnic literature or history courses? Should these courses be for members of a particular ethnic group? Should all students who enroll in a freshman English class have to read ethnic writers?
2. If classes focus on ethnic issues and are attended mainly by those most interested — members of those groups — might the classes tend to "ghettoize" minorities on campus?
3. Is a multicultural society an appropriate goal, or might we lose our American identity and values in such a society?

Depending on the student body, students may resent devoting a course to the immigrant and ethnic experience. Airing these concerns early on is one way to explain the purposes of the course and allow students to vent their feelings.

The Social Context for Writing

Before deciding on the organization of the class, you might consider the following factors that we believe can influence learning. We think it is important to create a comfortable, safe atmosphere for all students by validating their contributions to the class. In addition, you must be constantly on the alert to assess the learning situation for *all* students, both majority and minority. One reason we recommend small-group work and reader responses is that these activities tend to allow students to comment freely. Students often feel safer talking in a small group, out

of the instructor's hearing. Because there can be no "wrong" responses, students
will become more comfortable about their writing.

You should also consider creating a learning situation that will tap the expertise
of your students. The material presented in this text focuses on many cultures. In
some cases, your students may be more knowledgeable about those cultures than
you are. We hope that your class will provide opportunities for students who are
members of particular groups to share their specialized knowledge. However, you
should consider that a single minority student may be uncomfortable serving as
the "representative" of an entire group.

One natural response in reading about an unfamiliar culture is the forming of
generalizations and opinions about the culture as a whole. Thus, you should
caution students not to stereotype. A discussion of the individual variations that
occur within cultural boundaries will help students understand that while people
share a culture and its values, every person is different. When speculating about
the characteristics of a group, students who are members of that group can
comment on the validity of the speculations.

Material such as this may provoke controversial discussions. In such
discussions, it is important that students learn to listen to one another with
respect even if they disagree. You can model this behavior and reinforce it when it
occurs. In addition, if problems arise and tempers get out of hand, post-reading
class discussions about the breakdown in communication can clear the air and help
students understand the dynamics of the interaction. Sometimes this discussion
can take place immediately. In other cases, it is better to let tempers cool and have
the discussion at the next class meeting. When things go wrong, discussing them
openly nearly always works better than trying to ignore the problems and leave
resentment simmering.

An alternative approach is to have students write a journal entry about the
discussion — where misunderstandings occurred and so forth.

Enhancing the Learning Experience

Here we recommend some teaching strategies as well as additional activities we
believe will enrich the learning experience.

Active Reading   We hope that students will actively interact with the text by
outlining, taking notes, and using other strategies. One technique that works well
to further recall and analysis is "paragraph glossing." This strategy is particularly
helpful with a difficult reading and can be done in class or as a homework
assignment.

Paragraph glossing can be organized in the following ways. Working
individually or in pairs, students can gloss an entire essay or a single page or
paragraph. Then the individuals or pairs read the material and write a sentence
summarizing the content. For a classroom activity, individuals or pairs of students
can be assigned a page from the selection to gloss (students usually can gloss a
page in about five minutes). Then students read their glosses aloud or write them

on the board in sequence. This way the entire class can see an outline of the main ideas in a difficult piece of writing. The glosses also can provide a natural lead-in for discussion because students have chosen what they believe is important. Further, students can challenge one another's interpretations. For students who have difficulty reading complex pieces, this technique can enhance their ability to comprehend material, to see how an essay is put together, and to write their own essays.

Small-Group Activities   Small-group discussions and other collaborative reading and writing activities break the pattern of relying on teacher-directed activities, which often limit participation to a few (and usually the same) students. Instead, the class can be broken up into groups for discussion, for activities such as paragraph glossing or jigsawing (dividing reading material into parts, with each student in a group reading that part and then summarizing it for the other group members), or for collaborative writing assignments.

Groups can be formed at random. For example, students can form groups with students sitting next to them or with students working on the same essay topic. In classrooms with tables and movable chairs, small-group formation is easy; classrooms with fixed desks (anathema for the composition teacher) require more ingenuity. Students can even sit on tables or on the floor. Each group can be given the same or a different question orally or on a slip of paper. Usually the group or the instructor appoints one person to record the discussion and report on it at the end of the class. The instructor circulates to answer questions, listen in, and keep groups on task.

Small-group activities offer many benefits. They encourage shy students to participate. Also, students who participate in groups usually achieve a sense of the classroom as a writing community.

Reading Logs   We don't recommend tests in a composition classroom, because the courses themselves are so writing intensive. However, we do advocate reader response journals or reading logs. Reader response journals provide a way for students to write down their responses to a particular reading, therefore allowing them to formulate their ideas about the reading, react to it, and so forth. The journal can then be used as the basis for class discussion about the reading or as a place for working through ideas for more formal papers.

Reading logs can follow several formats. Students may write responses to each reading assignment of at least one page. A response can vary from a summary of the material, to a personal memory elicited by the reading, to the student's questions regarding the reading, to a formal analysis of the material. Usually the directions include asking students to notice something in the reading and respond to it. You might encourage students to relate a point made in the reading to a personal experience, analyze the point, or discuss it in a manner that demonstrates careful thinking about the issue raised. Sometimes responses focus on parts of the reading that moved or angered students. Help students report these responses and analyze why they responded as they did. Students can read their responses aloud in small groups and then use them to initiate discussion. You can collect the journals every week or two and read them. Responses are never graded or corrected for grammar or spelling. You can, however, make an overall comment, preferably addressed to the student by name and signed by you. Your comment might respond to questions, acknowledge the student's contribution, and perhaps include suggestions regarding content and development.

An additional method of using reader responses is to have students write a ten-minute response to the reading in class. Then circulate the responses so that everyone gets to read all of them. As you read the responses, you can note points to bring up in the following class discussion. Alternatively, responses can be circulated in small groups for discussion and then reported to the entire class.

Dialogue   Another way to begin discussion about a reading is through the use of a dialogue. Several questions in the text direct students to use this technique. A dialogue pairs students, usually at random, in the role of two authors, two characters in the reading and so on. You can begin the dialogue by writing the first few lines on the board. For example, in Myra Kelly's "A Soul Above Buttons" (Chapter 1), the teacher and the Boss might conduct a dialogue about school. The discussion might begin with the Boss saying, "I don't see no reason to learn to read and write." The first student in the pair is the Boss and writes from the Boss's point of view. The second student is the teacher and answers the remark as the teacher might. Then the paper is passed back to the student/Boss, who responds to the student/teacher's comment. Then the student/Boss returns the dialogue to the student/teacher. The students continue writing the dialogue for fifteen to twenty minutes. Finally, they read their creation aloud to the class. Students often are eager to read their own parts and infuse them with appropriate expression and inflection. The process indeed produces a lively class session.

You can also use the dialogue to discuss other issues that come up in class. For example, you can assign a dialogue between two "authors" in response to a point that comes up in discussion. Students really seem to enjoy the dialogue technique, and the result is a diversity of responses that would be unattainable in large-group discussions.

We hope you will feel free to experiment with these techniques and to vary them with your own and your students' needs. We also encourage you to allow students to design their own reading and writing activities.

PART TWO

CHAPTER NOTES

CHAPTER 1

EARLY IMMIGRANTS: LIVING IN AMERICA

This chapter chronicles the struggles of several representative groups of early immigrants to the East Coast of the United States. We chose to begin with the years 1880 to 1920 because this period was marked by a wave of immigration to the United States not only of Europeans but also of the first Arab immigrants. In addition, this period saw the beginning of the debate between the ideals of nativism and cultural pluralism. However, students should be reminded that there were many willing and unwilling immigrants to this country before the 1880s who, with the original inhabitants and later immigrants, make up the American mosaic.

The introduction to this chapter sets the scene for the reader by explaining the political and economic conditions in Europe and the Middle East that prompted the large wave of immigration. Reading the introduction will help students understand the mindset of the writers of the period, so they should read it before reading any of the selections. Many students — whether the great-grandchildren of the immigrants or descendants of established U.S. residents who found themselves facing new competition for jobs, housing, and power — will have some personal connection with immigrants of this period. By presenting the reasons for this wave of immigration and the conditions that met the new arrivals, the introduction may help students recall their own families' stories about the immigration experience.

One theme that emerges in the introduction and recurs throughout the book is assimilation. You may wish to begin exploring this topic here so that students can see how their opinions and awareness develop as they read through the text. When examining assimilation, you might discuss why some immigrants are highly motivated to enter the American mainstream whereas others are equally determined to retain their traditional ways. You also might contrast their situation with those of groups who were unwilling immigrants to the United States, such as Africans (brought as slaves), Native Americans (immigrants through conquest), and Mexicans (who suddenly found themselves living in the United States when territory changed hands). If time permits, students could be encouraged to interview family members and gather family stories or mementos to share with the class and lead into the Beginning exercise.

Beginning: Pre-reading/Writing

Working in a group, use the knowledge you have gained from reading the introduction to this chapter or your own experience to list the possible reasons that immigrants flocked to America during the period between 1880 and 1920. Share your list with the class. How do you think these reasons compare with those motivating immigrants today?

We recommend setting aside one class period for this discussion to set up the context for reading the whole chapter. We like dividing the class into small groups and letting each group speculate about reasons for emigrating. One source of information for the discussion would be the introduction. Another rich source would be students' own knowledge. Some students might remember facts from a history class. Others might have talked to parents and grandparents about why their families came to America.

Next, students could discuss what they think was particularly appealing about America as a destination. Again the introduction is one resource. But have students speculate about the political, economic, and social conditions that existed in this country in 1880. If students generate questions such as who was president, what were the immigration policies, and so forth, they can find the answers in the school library before the next class meeting. Different classes will take the discussion in different directions, and this should be encouraged. Native American or African American students might bring up their own history in America (which, of course, pre-dates this period). If students themselves don't introduce this issue, you might point out the contrast between immigrants who chose to come to "The Promised Land" and those who were forced to come to live as slaves or those who already were here and felt threatened by the newcomers.

Finally, one member of each group can summarize the group's discussion for the class while you or a student records the main points on the board. This list can then be used as the basis for a general discussion. This exercise can lead into the discussion of the Bill of Rights, undoubtedly one factor that made coming to America so appealing.

The Bill of Rights

The Bill of Rights, added to the Constitution in 1791, is a clear statement of the rights guaranteed to American citizens. To many immigrants who were fleeing repressive regimes or religious persecution, the Bill of Rights represented the ideal of freedom associated with America. For this reason, we chose the Bill of Rights as the beginning selection in the text. Other selections report numerous violations of the rights guaranteed as well as several incidents in which the Bill of Rights served to protect minority groups. If students are familiar with the Bill of Rights, they will better understand the struggles of various groups to preserve these rights.

As a pre-reading assignment, you might ask students to write out as many of the provisions of the Bill of Rights as they know. Then they can compare their lists with the actual document. For a post-reading discussion, you can have students contrast the Bill of Rights with the protection afforded citizens in any of the European countries during the 1800s. In countries that offered ample protection of citizens' rights (Great Britain, for example), the motivation for emigrating probably was economic.

If students have trouble internalizing the meaning of the articles, you might ask them to write for ten minutes on question 1. If students are ready for a more complex assignment, you can use question 2 as a post-reading activity. It asks students to move away from the literal meaning of the Bill of Rights and speculate on the document's significance in a more specific context. The in-class writing or discussion can serve as a pre-writing activity for a formal essay. You might ask students why the Bill of Rights was an incentive for emigration. Then students' responses could be read aloud and used as the basis for further discussion.

♦ Responding

1. Explain in your own words what one of the provisions in the Bill of Rights guarantees or implies.

2. Choose one of the rights guaranteed in the Bill of Rights. Then, using information in the introduction to the chapter and your own knowledge, explain why that right was particularly important to early immigrants.

CONSTANTINE PANUNZIO
In the American Storm

In this selection from his book *The Soul of an Immigrant*, Panunzio recounts his harrowing experiences when he first arrived in America from Italy. As a pre-reading activity, you can set the scene by asking students to imagine that they have just arrived in a strange country with little money, poor knowledge of the language, and no job or place to stay. Ask them to brainstorm about how they would feel, and list their responses on the board. Then, after reading the selection, students can begin discussion by comparing their responses to Panunzio's.

If you use this pre-reading activity, questions 2, 3, and 4 can be helpful as post-reading activities. Question 2 asks students to continue focusing on Panunzio's experiences while encouraging them to think about their own responses and explain why they made their choices. Question 4 continues to focus on the story as a stimulus for personal writing, but it requires an understanding and summary of Panunzio's experiences and some analysis of students' own or their families' experiences. Because this question is personal, students have a lot of leeway. For example, they might compare Panunzio's experience with their own experiences upon first leaving home for college. This might work well as either a journal entry or a formal paper.

If you want to examine the themes of this reading rather than elicit personal responses, question 1 would work as an in-class post-reading activity. Working in groups, students can list examples of Panunzio's stormy early experiences. They can share the examples in class and then use them as the basis for discussion or a formal essay.

Question 3 requires more outside knowledge but can help develop a more thorough understanding of the period. As such, it might work well in a class discussion which would tap the resources of many students and the instructor. Alternatively, it can provide a topic for students who want to do additional research.

Other readings with similar themes of arrival and settling in a new country include Sung (Chapter 2), Yamamoto (Chapter 5), and Mathabane and Hijuelos (Chapter 9).

♦ Responding

1. Using examples from Panunzio's autobiography, illustrate how the storm he encountered on his journey was "indeed prophetic of [his] early experiences in America."

2. What working conditions made life particularly unbearable for Panunzio? What would you have found most intolerable?

3. Panunzio arrived in Boston in 1902, almost one hundred years ago. How have employment opportunities and working conditions for immigrants changed since then?

4. Compare Panunzio's experiences in a new situation and country with the experiences your family had when they first came to the United States or when they moved to another part of the country, or with your own experiences in a new environment.

JACOB RIIS
Genesis of the Tenement

We have included this excerpt from Riis's book to give students a sense of conditions in New York City during this period and the forces that created those conditions. Further sense of the period can be obtained from the pictures in the text. A pre-reading discussion might begin by looking at the picture of the crowded streets of New York and having students write a short in-class description of what they see. The post-reading activity might elicit parallels between the tenements of that period and conditions faced by residents of today's housing projects or by the homeless. As students read further in the chapter, you might ask them to consider which immigrants they would expect to find inhabiting Riis's tenements.

Questions 1 and 3 try to raise students' awareness of the conditions during Riis's time and those in urban areas today. Bearing in mind current conditions in the projects or with the homeless, one issue students might want to consider is whether or not life is truly better for today's immigrants and the poor now than it was in Riis's time.

Students who live in rural areas or urban students from relatively affluent neighborhoods may be unaware of the squalid living conditions that exist in many poor urban areas. Students who come from poorer families may be invited to share stories about their communities (but they should not be pressured to do so). Another resource is the media.

Questions 2 and 4 ask students to think about the issue of landlord responsibility. Recently some slumlords have been in the public eye because they have been sentenced to live in their own slums. Students can compare ideas about landlord responsibility in our time with those at the turn of the century.

♦ Responding

1. Compare Riis's description of the New York tenements of the 1880s to any part of your own or a nearby city today.

2. Working individually or in a group, list the rights and responsibilities of landlords and tenants. Whose rights have primary importance if there is a conflict? Share your lists in class.

3. Consider the statement that "experts had testified that, as compared with uptown, rents were from twenty-five to thirty per cent higher in the worst slums of the lower wards." How do you account for that difference? Compare that situation to conditions in a city you know. Are rents, goods, and services more expensive in poor neighborhoods than in middle-class or rich neighborhoods?

4. Riis quotes a report on slum conditions that says, "The proprietors frequently urged the filthy habits of the tenants as an excuse for the condition of their property, utterly losing sight of the fact that it was the tolerance of those habits which was the real evil, and that for this they themselves were alone responsible." Do you agree or disagree?

OLE EDVART ROLVAAG
Facing the Great Desolation

This excerpt is interesting because it presents a reluctant pioneer, Beret, who, unlike so many heroines of film and story, wishes she were elsewhere and has great difficulty adjusting to life on the prairie. Her husband, on the other hand, thrives on the adventure, traveling around while she is left to cope with the house and children. It's not surprising that she loses control.

Beret's struggles with self-control and loneliness and with external elements as she attempts to create a community in the wilderness are possible themes for exploration and discussion. This excerpt highlights the special difficulties for both male and female immigrants. If you wish to concentrate on the issue of gender, a pre-reading activity might ask students to discuss the different challenges faced by men and women. The post-reading discussion might focus around question 1, which deals with gender roles within the culture during this period. It is important that students see this family in its cultural context and understand that gender roles were culture specific.

If you wish to explore the unique difficulties new immigrants faced in becoming pioneers, you might use a pre-reading assignment that asks students to brainstorm about the pressures all pioneers experienced. For a post-reading exercise, questions 2 and 3 can help in examining the pressures on Beret and Per Hansa and the different ways each dealt with difficulties. This could lead into question 4, which asks students to compare Beret with the stereotypical pioneer heroine.

Other readings with the theme of women challenged by circumstances are Yezierska in this chapter and Mohr (Chapter 4).

◆ Responding

1. Although still young, Ole and Store-Hans have already internalized traditional roles and attitudes about gender. Using the evidence in the reading, list the behaviors and duties they expect from males and females.

2. Analyze Beret's responses to the boys' fight. What pressures produced her reaction? What was she thinking and feeling when she "left the child screaming in the middle of the floor, went out of the house, and was gone a long time"? Pretend you are Beret and write an entry in your diary about the event.

3. Compare Beret's and Per Hansa's attitudes to life in the wilderness. How do you account for the differences? Some factors to consider are personal temperament, gender, upbringing, activities, responsibilities, ambitions, and expectations for the future.

4. Beret has great difficulty dealing with life on the prairie. Using your own knowledge, describe the pioneer heroine often portrayed in stories and films. Compare her character and behavior with Beret's.

MYRA KELLY
A Soul Above Buttons

Our students enjoy this story because of the contrast between the Boss's and the teacher's assumptions and expectations. It invites discussion about the goals of education — a recurring theme throughout this book. As a pre-reading question, you might ask students to think about these goals as the topic of a ten-minute in-class writing assignment. Using the dialogue assignment as a post-reading activity (see question 1) would lead to further discussion of these goals. As part of a follow-up discussion, students may want to consider the relationship between the way people speak and how society treats them.

The dialogue assignment in question 1 can produce some interesting and imaginative results as well as generate questions about the values of education. Students could use that discussion as pre-writing for a more formal paper based on question 4.

Question 2 would also help focus the post-reading discussion. After defining the terms, students might consider which type of "smart" is more beneficial to the Boss in his situation and to themselves. Should the Boss have stayed in school? Should the school have adjusted the curriculum to meet his perceived needs?

If your class is comfortable with reading aloud or "acting," the dramatization suggested in question 3 will be illuminating. The comparison can be written or oral.

◆ Responding

1. Working with a partner, write a dialogue in which one of you, pretending to be the Boss, complains that the curriculum is not relevant, and the other, pretending to be Miss Bailey, tries to convince the Boss to remain in school. Read the dialogue aloud to the class.

2. Define "street smart" and "book smart." Use characters and examples from the story and from your own experience to illustrate your definitions.

3. Part of the humor in this story comes from the different assumptions and expectations of the Boss and Miss Bailey. Read aloud or act out some of the scenes between the two characters. Analyze the class's spontaneous response. Compare these situations with other "fish-out-of-water" stories, such as the films *Crocodile Dundee I* and *II* and Mark Twain's *A Connecticut Yankee in King Arthur's Court.*

4. Miss Bailey defines the goal of education as teaching "those things which will help make you useful when you are big and to keep you happy while you are little." Compare her goals with your personal educational goals.

ANZIA YEZIERSKA
The Fat of the Land

We find this story very touching. Students, however, might have a harder time identifying with the mother than we do. Readers need to sympathize with Hanneh Breineh to appreciate her predicament at the end of the story, but they also must understand how she treated the children when they were young and the effect this had on their relationships. Again some pre-reading activity might be useful. The Riis excerpt is a good resource; class discussion might focus on the conditions new immigrants to New York faced and the difficulties of raising a large family on a meager income. A discussion about what such a family might wish for in the future would prepare the class for the ironic turn of events.

Your students might need help with pronunciation of characters' names as well as the Yiddish words. A dictionary will provide pronunciations, or perhaps someone in the class will have that expertise. You may also want to point out to your students that Yezierska translates the Yiddish curses verbatim and that they suffer in translation.

A post-reading discussion can center around Hanneh's relationship with her children both before and after "making it." Working in groups, students could discuss to what extent the distance between the mother and children was caused by Hanneh's treatment of them when they were young or by her insistence on clinging to her old ways when they are older. Questions 1, 2, and 3 explore these different angles.

Question 2 asks students to take the viewpoint of one of the other characters in the story. The letter format often is effective because it allows the writer to become part of a rhetorical situation and enables him or her to visualize the audience.

If you discussed the issue of poverty and what a family like the Breinehs might aspire to during pre-reading, question 4 could be used as a short in-class writing assignment to begin a post-reading discussion. Since the idea of "making it" occurs throughout the text, the drafts could later be expanded into longer essays possibly comparing the Breinehs' experience with those of other immigrant families, such as in Hijuelos' "Visitors, 1965" (Chapter 9).

Another post-reading discussion might begin by relating Hanneh's situation to Beret's in "Facing the Great Desolation," pointing up the difficulties for female immigrants in general and mothers of small children in particular. Students might also want to consider the psychological effect on Hanneh of being no longer needed after having been forced to be so resourceful in her younger days.

Readings with a similar theme of mother/daughter conflict and embarrassment about holding onto tradition and wishing to become part of the mainstream include Cofer (Chapter 4) and Walker (Chapter 9).

♦ Responding

1. Compare Hanneh Breineh's life before and after her husband's death. Consider both her physical and emotional circumstances.

2. We see Hanneh Breineh from the author's sympathetic point of view, but the other characters in the story view her differently. Imagine that you are one of her children and write a letter to a friend explaining your mother's behavior. Or write a journal entry about a time when you were torn between loyalty to a parent, sibling, or friend and embarrassment about that person's behavior in front of someone you wanted to impress.

3. Hanneh Breineh learns something in this story. "She had fled from the marble sepulcher of the Riverside apartment to her old home in the ghetto; but now she knew that she could not live there again. She had outgrown her past by the habits of years of physical comforts, and these material comforts that she could no longer do without choked and crushed the life within her." Working individually or in a group, write a moral to this story, then share it with the class.

4. Hanneh Breineh's friend and old neighbor Mrs. Pelz says that in America money is everything: "What greater friend is there on earth than the dollar?" She believes that the only trouble with Hanneh Breineh is that she "got it too good." Do you agree or disagree? Support your argument with evidence from the story as well as from your own experience.

GREGORY ORFALEA
Who Am I? The Syrians Dock in America

We were especially pleased to include this excerpt from Orfalea's book in this section on early immigrants because, as the reading points out, the large number of Syrians who immigrated to the United States in 1883 generally have been ignored. The excerpt also discusses the experience of immigrants at Ellis Island. A pre-reading activity might include asking students if any members of their families entered the United States through Ellis Island. Alternatively, students might share what Ellis Island means to them using information from the introduction to the chapter, the reading itself, and their own prior knowledge.

In a post-reading discussion, questions 1 and 2 would help focus attention on the characteristics of the Syrian immigrants. Because Orfalea emphasizes that they were overlooked, students might want to spend some time discussing what made these immigrants different from other immigrant groups in the United States. Question 4 gives students another opportunity to share their immigrant backgrounds; for example, Native American students might discuss the impact of the immigrant wave on their ancestors' situations.

Because this is the only reading that reports the experience of immigrants at Ellis Island, you and your students may want to examine the conflicting aspects of the port of entry and analyze the government's response. A debate on the exclusion policy could be a logical outgrowth of such an exploration. After discussing or debating the issue, students could use the information from the reading, the introduction to the chapter, and the debate to write a formal essay.

♦ Responding

1. Explain the basis of Orfalea's observation that the Syrians who arrived at Ellis Island in 1883 seemed as unknown in 1983 as they were a century back.

2. Using specific examples from the reading, explain why poet Amin Rishani called "the pathway of the immigrant a virtual 'Via Dolorosa' with the Stations of the Cross Beirut, Marseilles, and Ellis Island."

3. For some immigrants, Ellis Island was an "Island of Tears"; for others, "the house of freedom." Explain the significance of the two names, and discuss the selection process that took place at Ellis Island. Was the American government too harsh in its treatment of arriving immigrants? What rationale might there have been for the selection process?

4. Working in a group, share family stories of immigration to the United States. List all of the different places you know of where people entered the country. Share your list with the class.

DAVID M. FINE
Attitudes Toward Acculturation in the English Fiction of the Jewish Immigrant, 1900–1917

This essay, like the final essays in each chapter, reflects on issues brought up by writers of the period from a contemporary perspective. The essay may be difficult for students, so you might assign collaborative or individual paragraph glossing. A possible pre-reading assignment is to have students discuss their ideas about the term "melting pot." They can review its origin (described in the introduction to the chapter) and discuss the image of America it presents.

After reading the selection, students can go on to discuss cultural pluralism and the problems minorities face when they are pressured to renounce their own languages and cultures and assimilate. To facilitate such a discussion, you may want to look at questions 1, 2, and 3, which deal with the issues of assimilation and the melting pot versus cultural pluralism. Since each of these questions addresses the melting-pot issue from a different angle, the class might choose to divide into groups to work collaboratively on an answer to one question. Alternatively, students might choose one question as a topic for a formal paper.

Question 4 introduces a theme that recurs throughout the text: the difficulties that sometimes arise between assimilated or acculturated immigrants and new immigrants. Students should be made aware of the intolerance former immigrants or their children often exhibit toward new immigrants.

The themes of acculturation and assimilation also appear in Mura (Chapter 9).

♦ Responding

1. An important issue that is still controversial is whether immigrants should strive for assimilation or maintain cultural pluralism. Working individually or in a group, define the two concepts. Write an essay discussing the implications of each for the individual immigrant. Support your points with examples from the readings or from your own knowledge and experience.

2. Using information from Fine's article, define and trace the history of the term "melting pot." How might critics object to the image of America as a melting pot? What other image might replace it?

3. How does the melting-pot image, which many Americans have advocated for years, fit into a society that wants to encourage cultural diversity? Write an essay arguing that America should or should not try to be a melting pot.

4. Fine introduces Sidney Nyburg's *The Chosen People* as "a vehicle for examining the broader question of the cultural gulf between older and newer Americans in the early years of the twentieth century." Describe this gulf. Does a similar gulf exist between established Americans and new immigrants today?

CONNECTING (printed in AMERICAN MOSAIC, p. 87)

Critical Thinking and Writing

The connecting questions can be used in several ways. You might want to use them to integrate and sum up the chapter. They can serve as discussion topics or as the topics for formal essays. We recommend that you let your students choose the questions they wish to write about or let them use these questions as models for ones that they will design themselves. The connecting questions usually cover a broader scope than the Responding questions that follow each reading. These either ask students to relate large issues within the chapter or across the text. If you are using a thematic approach, these questions will help students to trace themes throughout the text.

If you want students to consider connections within this chapter, refer them to questions 6 and 7. If students are ready to compare readings across the text, have them consider questions 1, 2, 3, 4, and 9. For questions that focus on broad general issues see questions 4, 8, and 12.

If you have students who want to deal with topics that require library research, more extensive questions dealing with specific legal and social issues are provided in the section entitled for further research.

CHAPTER 2

CHINESE IMMIGRANTS: THE LURE OF THE GOLD MOUNTAIN

This chapter deals with the immigration of the Chinese to America that began in the 1840s. Students should read the introduction first, because it will help them understand the complex situation the Chinese immigrants faced. On the one hand, they were encouraged to come to America and praised for their hard work; on the other, many forces were at work to keep them out. These forces ultimately led to the passage of the Exclusion Act and also prevented the Chinese already in the country from attaining citizenship.

Beginning: Pre-reading/Writing

Working in a group, use the knowledge of early Chinese immigrants you have gained from the introduction to this chapter, other books or media, and personal experience to try to construct profiles of some of the first Chinese immigrants in California. Consider sex, age, marital status, economic status, skills or profession, and reasons for immigrating. Share your profile with the class. What kind of person do you think would have made the journey from China to a foreign land in the mid-1800s?

The Beginning Pre-reading/Writing assignment asks students to flesh out the portrait of the early Chinese immigrants. The goal of the assignment is to make students aware of the hardships these immigrants endured and think about what would motivate them to attempt such a difficult journey. Because students will discover that these immigrants were ambitious and hard working, they should question the reasons why this group was excluded in 1882. This can lead to a discussion of the Exclusion Act, with a focus on why some minority groups are perceived as a threat by the majority.

From The Chinese Exclusion Act

This excerpt depicts Americans' fear of the Chinese. As a pre-reading activity, you might discuss how the Chinese immigrants' resistance to assimilation and the "collective resolve" of the Chinese community may have contributed to the fear.

You also could discuss how a nation might justify legalizing discrimination. Still another option would be to assign question 1 as a pre-reading activity and have students come to class with information from the library.

If you don't use question 1 as a pre-reading assignment, three groups can quickly answer the three parts of question 1. The groups can then pool their information and go on to questions 2 and 3.

Question 3 can serve as the topic of a short in-class writing assignment. Students might want to imagine that they are immigrants from another (perhaps Asian) country who hear about the Chinese Exclusion Act and discuss its effect, if any, on their decision to immigrate to America. Students may also want to discuss how the act conflicts with the image of America presented by the Bill of Rights (Chapter 1).

♦ Responding

1. Using material from the introduction to the chapter, your own knowledge, or sources in your school library, gather information to answer the following questions.
   a. Why were the Chinese invited to the United States in the 1800s?
   b. How many laborers were imported from China?
   c. What projects did they primarily work on?

2. Working individually or in a group, use the information gained from your research into the importation of laborers to speculate about the reactions of other groups already in the West.

3. Discuss the ways in which the Exclusion Act of 1882 tried to curtail Chinese immigration. What effect did the passage of this act have on the image of America as a land of opportunity?

BETTY LEE SUNG
The Pioneer Chinese

Sung describes the early Chinese immigrants to America, their reasons for leaving their homeland, and the reactions of family members remaining in China. Her discussion of these factors illustrates the interplay of social and economic factors that contributed to the decision to emigrate. Since students were asked to consider all of these factors when they wrote their profiles for the Beginning exercise, a possible pre-reading activity is to have them review their profiles. As they read the selection, they can compare their profiles to the people Sung describes.

If your students want to discuss reasons for immigration, question 1 is a good place to start. Though it calls on students to look back at the text, it also allows them to speculate.

A short in-class writing assignment based on question 2 would allow students to look closely at the Chinese immigrant experience.

Question 3 aims to expand students' understanding of the role of the Chinese community in helping new immigrants settle. You might discuss how the success of the community may have bred resentment and opposition to the Chinese that culminated in the Exclusion Act.

One natural response to reading about an unfamiliar culture is to form generalizations and opinions about the culture as a whole. Question 4 asks students to use these readings as the basis for generalizations about Chinese culture and character. However, students should be cautioned not to stereotype. A discussion of the variations among individuals that exist within cultural boundaries would help students understand that while people may share a culture and its values, every person is different. Note that question 4 asks students to list the values that "seemed to be important." Therefore, you should stress that they will be speculating from minimal evidence. If you have any Chinese American or Chinese immigrant students in your class, you might ask them to comment on the validity of the speculations.

Other readings that examine the reception of new immigrants are Panunzio (Chapter 1), Yamamoto (Chapter 5), and Hijuelos (Chapter 9).

◆ Responding

1. Discuss the lure that attracted early Chinese immigrants to America. Why were so many anxious to come to San Francisco in spite of the dangers involved in leaving China?

2. Fatt Hing's experience is presented as typical of that of many Chinese immigrants. Outline the main events that characterized his life as an immigrant.

3. Chairman Wong says, "One valuable lesson we have learned and which you will soon appreciate is that we must stick together and help one another, even though we are not kin." Write an essay explaining the ways in which early Chinese immigrants helped later immigrants.

4. According to the reading, what aspects of Chinese culture and character helped the immigrants become successful in America? After isolating those characteristics, list the values that seemed to be important in Chinese culture. Compare these values to your own. Are these values important to you? To contemporary American society?

From The Gold Mountain Poems

The image of these anonymous Chinese immigrant writers expressing their disillusionment with America by writing poems on a wall is a poignant one. One approach to these poems is to look at writing as a way of dealing with frustration. Another is to examine the causes of frustration as disillusionment. As a pre-reading assignment, you might have students discuss what they do when they are upset, angry, or frustrated. This could lead to a discussion about how writing offers a way to deal with those feelings. Reading the poems aloud is an effective way to convey the emotions they express. A different student should read each poem to emphasize that each one was most likely written by a different author. You might discuss the language of the poems: how does it communicate frustration and hopelessness? Question 4 presents a possible follow-up to this approach, asking students to take advantage of this form of expression. A side discussion about graffiti (are graffiti destruction or expression?) might follow.

If you choose to examine the causes of the frustration, you might have a pre-reading discussion about the conflicting messages the United States presented. It encouraged the Chinese to come here when cheap labor was needed, then excluded them when they were perceived as a threat. Is it not ironic that a country would have both the Bill of Rights and the Exclusion Act? Question 1 is a good starting point for a discussion after reading any of the poems. You might ask whether the writers' feelings were justified. Was the United States government responsible for the immigrants' expectations? These questions could serve as pre-writing for an assignment based on question 3, which asks students to be analytical and persuasive. You might also have pairs of students write a dialogue as preparation, with one student acting as an immigrant and the other as an official.

The poems present a specific example of the helplessness and frustrations felt by later Chinese immigrants described in the introduction to the chapter. The next reading deals with the same theme and might be taught along with the poems.

♦ Responding

1. Describe the attitude of the speaker in any of the poems. How does he feel about the United States government?

2. We don't know why the speaker in these poems is imprisoned. Write your own story about the circumstances that might have caused him to be "deported to this island, like a convicted criminal."

3. Write a letter from a government official to a San Francisco newspaper justifying the speaker's imprisonment. Alternatively, write an editorial for a San Francisco newspaper condemning the treatment of prisoners held on Angel Island.

4. Unlike most of the poetry in this book, these poems were not written by
    professional poets who wanted to publish their work, but by immigrants who
    used poetry as a way of understanding their experiences and expressing their
    feelings. Write a poem about some experience that affected you strongly, or
    write a journal entry discussing the benefits of writing as an emotional outlet.

SUI SIN FAR
In the Land of the Free

This is one of the earliest stories by an Asian American writer. However, her
credentials as an expert on Asian life are somewhat suspect because, although her
mother was Chinese, her father was English, and she was raised in America. Her
sister, also an author, adopted a Japanese pseudonym. Her life is shrouded in
mystery; even her obituary contained misleading information. The family seemed
to be trying to hide her Asian heritage. Only recently, through research by S. E.
Solberg, have we obtained a clearer image. Nevertheless, Sin's work is important
because she is one of the first Americans to write from an Asian perspective.

   This story illustrates the injustices in the immigration system faced by later
Chinese immigrants. A pre-reading discussion might focus on the rights of parents
to bring immigrant children to the United States. A broader question would be
whether families should have the right to immigrate together. If they must be
separated, what effect would the separation have on family members?

   Another pre-reading discussion could focus on how intimidating it is to
encounter red tape in a new country with a different language and rules that don't
make sense. After reading, question 2 can prompt students to consider the
difficulties faced by people who must deal with government officials and their
vulnerability to exploitation by unscrupulous individuals. Students might compare
the problems of later Chinese immigrants to the reception the pioneer Chinese
received or to recent immigration stories. Such a discussion might serve as pre-
writing for question 4.

   If your students are more interested in the theme of loss of culture and identity,
they may want to discuss or write about question 3. This theme recurs throughout
the text, especially in the context of parent-child relationships. Some students may
have experienced or be experiencing the same fears and may be willing to discuss
their feelings with the class. Others may feel more comfortable discussing this
issue in relation to the story rather than to personal experience.

♦ Responding

1. Explain the irony of the title.

2. Analyze the motivation and behavior of James Clancy. Do you think he is
    sincerely trying to help Hom Hing? He hesitates before taking the jewels in

payment for his services. What do you think is going through his mind at that moment? Why does he accept them as payment? What do you think he should have done?

3. In what ways might the story represent the fears of loss of culture and identity that plague many new immigrants to the United States?

4. Although the language and writing style of this story are dated, the theme of being caught in the trap of official bureaucracy is current. Rewrite the story with a contemporary setting. Alternatively, write about a time when you or someone you know had to fight what seemed to be endless red tape.

PARDEE LOWE
Father Cures a Presidential Fever

In this excerpt from his biography of his father, Lowe describes his disillusionment upon finding that the American Dream was not a reality for the Chinese. However, you may want to inform students that throughout the biography itself, there is both an expression of faith in the potential for success in the new country and a respect for the rituals and customs that comprised his family's cultural heritage. Your students probably will easily relate to this reading, because it presents a number of issues that many of them are exploring: the struggle to realize unrealistic dreams, the disillusionment of discovering that the world is not just, parental versus one's own expectations, and the realization that some things are out of one's control.

A pre- or post-reading discussion could focus on what students know about the American Dream and whether they accept that image of America. After reading, students may wish to look at question 1, which asks them first to restate the facts of the story and then to evaluate the opportunities that would be open to Lowe or to other minorities today. This may provoke a controversial discussion, with some students insisting that racism is nonexistent and others claiming that American society is completely racist. In such a discussion, it is important to help students learn to listen to one another with respect even if they don't agree. You can model this behavior and reinforce it when it occurs. In addition, if problems arise and tempers get out of hand, a post-reading class discussion about the breakdown in communication can clear the air and help students understand the dynamics of the interaction. You can have this discussion immediately or wait until tempers cool and have it at the next class meeting, depending on the mood of the class. An alternative is to have students write a journal entry about the discussion — where misunderstandings occurred and so forth. When things go wrong, discussing them openly often works much better than trying to ignore problems and leaving some students feeling resentful.

Another approach is to have a pre-reading discussion that focuses on students' childhood dreams and how students' abilities and choices, as well as the limitations imposed on them by family, economic circumstances, or society, have limited their options. A post-reading discussion could focus on the choices Lowe made to promote his chances for the presidency and the limits he faced both within and outside of his family. How did his efforts to get a summer job and so forth increase the frustration brought on by prejudice?

A variation on this theme would be to focus a pre-reading discussion on the dreams students' parents have for them and how they conflict with their own dreams. After reading the selection, students can follow this up with question 3, comparing how Lowe and his father handled the conflict with the way they and their parents resolve conflicts.

Question 2 repeats the issue of preserving one's culture through an assignment on the difficulties of being a member of two cultures. Students who are part of the majority culture need to be made aware of the difficulties members of minority groups encounter when they try to live in two cultures at once. This question could also be discussed in class as a pre-writing exercise.

Questions 3 and 4 deal with Lowe's role in the Chinese family during this period. Students should be made aware of some general aspects of Chinese culture but also be cautioned not to stereotype. Chinese American students could serve as resources for information about traditional Chinese family structures.

Other readings that deal with the conflict of maintaining one's identity in two cultures are Okada (Chapter 5), Mora (Chapter 7), Allen (Chapter 8), and Hagedorn (Chapter 9).

♦ Responding

1. Explain what happens to Pardee Lowe to change his original optimism about equal opportunity in America to an understanding that in post–World War I San Francisco there would never be an opening for him with an American company and that, as he says in the story, he didn't have "a 'Chinaman's chance' of becoming President of the United States." What opportunities would be open to Pardee Lowe today? Could he be elected President of the United States?

2. Discuss the problems Pardee Lowe has in being a "filial Chinese son and good American citizen at one and the same time." Do you agree that it is difficult to be a part of two cultures? In writing your essay, use the reading as well as the experiences of you and your friends to support your argument.

3. Lowe's father holds certain hopes and aspirations for his son. Compare those with the aspirations he holds for himself.

4. Working individually or in a group, list the roles and responsibilities of the members of the extended Lowe family. Share your list with the class. Write an essay comparing this family with other families presented in this book or with your own family.

MAXINE HONG KINGSTON
The Grandfather of the Sierra Nevada Mountains

This essay, which combines factual and fictionalized episodes, reflects on the experiences of the Chinese who built the railroads from a modern perspective, thus serving to explode the stereotype. Rather than presenting the romanticized vision of happy workers, Kingston outlines the grim reality and danger that faced men like her grandfather. She also explores how these men suffered loneliness and loss of identity. Your students probably are unaware of the massacres of Chinese workers (which went unpunished), so you may want to bring this up before they read the selection.

Question 1 focuses on an important aspect of this reading: the contributions of the Chinese to America. Whether or not students choose to write on this topic, it could serve as a follow-up small- or large-group discussion topic. You should remind students that Kingston's grandfather couldn't become an American citizen because Asians were unable to obtain citizenship. How was it possible that the United States, home of the Bill of Rights and the Constitution, could deny citizenship to a particular group? Students need to remember that despite this protection, slavery had been legal until the 1860s.

Question 2 focuses on context, asking students to acknowledge the importance of time and place in shaping events. You should point out that each writer in both this chapter and the remaining text (as in any text) was writing in a particular time and place. A comparison of Sung and Kingston would illustrate this point. By highlighting the dreadful safety record in the mines and on the railways and the hatred and violence visited on the workers, the piece presents a vivid contrast to the brighter picture Sung paints. A comparison of the two portrayals might be a topic for a post-reading discussion. Students could consider when each was written and the attitudes toward Chinese Americans in each period. How did the circumstances of time and place influence each piece? Was Kingston freer to bemoan past conditions because minorities feel less reluctant to report on negative aspects of their histories in America now than they did in the 1960s? Does Sung whitewash history and play down the negatives to appeal to the majority or to avoid offending those in power?

Question 3 offers students the opportunity to be creative with the facts and explore the motivation of both sides. Can anything justify the Boss's actions?

◆ Responding

1. Maxine Hong Kingston calls her grandfather "an American ancestor, a holding, homing ancestor of this place," even though he was never legally an American citizen. Explain his contribution to this country.

2. Working in a group, discuss the ways in which Kingston's grandfather's life was shaped by the place where he was living and the opportunities available to him. Write a journal entry or an essay about the ways in which you or any of your relatives have been directly affected by the period or place in which you happen to be born or live.

3. Imagine that you are a reporter for a San Francisco newspaper in the late 1800s. You have just returned from interviewing Chinese railroad workers. Write a feature story for your newspaper arguing that they are being exploited and mistreated by the "demon" bosses, or write a story from the bosses' point of view about working conditions on the railroad.

4. Choose one of the atrocities Kingston writes about and expand your knowledge of the circumstances by researching the incident in your school library. Write your own version and share it with the class.

CONNECTING (printed in AMERICAN MOSAIC, p. 159)

Critical Thinking and Writing

The connecting questions relate readings to each other both within the chapter and throughout the text. For some strategies on using them in the classroom, see the comments in chapter 1 of the manual. In this set of questions, number 1 asks students to use material from the chapter to discuss a larger issue while 2, 3, 4, and 5 direct students to other chapters.

If students have read Chapter 1, they might want to look at questions 7, 8, 9, and 10 which relate directly to issues raised in that chapter.

Question 6 is a general question that can be answered with examples from this chapter, other chapters, or outside information.

Though the research questions usually require outside reading, research question 1 might be answered with information from this text.

CHAPTER 3

AFRICAN AMERICANS: THE MIGRATION NORTH AND THE HARLEM RENAISSANCE

This chapter covers the important period of the Harlem Renaissance. Students should learn about the changes that were taking place in the United States during the great migration of African Americans north. This coincided with a period of increasing racial awareness and, for African Americans, a turning toward an African aesthetic. The introduction to the chapter examines some of the reasons behind the migration and sets the scene for the articles. Students need to grasp the context to understand Locke's article, which explains the rationale behind this renaissance.

Beginning: Pre-reading/Writing

What's in a name? A great deal, especially if it's the name of a group you belong to. Discuss why the name of an ethnic group is a particularly sensitive issue for people within that group. Consider the ways in which ethnic group names are chosen. Who does the naming, and who uses the name? Why do groups sometimes decide that they prefer to be called by a new name? For example, why was the name Negro rejected by the African American community? What are the psychological effects of names with positive or negative connotations? Why are some names appropriate when used by group members but not when used by outsiders?

The Beginning exercise focuses on names, which is certain to be a controversial issue in reading this chapter. Many authors of this period used the terms *Negro* and *nigger*. Before students read the selections in this chapter, a class discussion about historical uses of perjorative names and the pain they can inflict on *all* individuals might help ease students' discomfort at seeing such names in print.

Input from our African American students indicates that they don't object to discussing such names as long as derogatory terms for other groups are discussed as well. You might also contrast the passive role of being named by others and the active role of choosing a name. Who has the real power in such situations? This discussion could also examine personal preferences for names. Some have discarded the term *black* for *African American*. Others prefer to retain *black*, pointing out that they are not from Africa. (One of our students objected to the term *Afro-American*: "There's no such country as 'Afro.'") Some older African Americans continue to refer to themselves as *colored*. Obviously, this is a rich, albeit controversial, topic.

From The Constitution of South Carolina

This excerpt is representative of the many laws that disfranchised African Americans. Such laws prompted many African Americans to leave their homes in the South and move north. Students may want to know what happened to these provisions; this may lead to a discussion of the Civil Rights and Voting Rights Acts. You might emphasize how having those laws on the books for so many years impacted on people living in that part of the country. Students may want to read the introduction to Chapter 6, "The Struggle for Civil Rights," at this time.

As a pre-reading question, you could discuss what the right to vote means, both psychologically and in terms of power. After reading the excerpt, students may need to use question 1 to fully understand how South Carolina was able to nullify the Fifteenth Amendment. If you choose to look at question 2, which asks how certain citizens were disfranchised, you may want to ask students to discuss why the government attempted to take this action. Students might discuss the Exclusion Act here.

Question 3 may lead to a broader discussion about why additional legislation was needed to supplement the Bill of Rights.

♦ Responding

1. Find the provisions in this section of the constitution of South Carolina that could be used to keep someone from voting. Who has the discretion to grant someone the right to vote?

2. Working in a group, discuss the ways in which the power structure in a society can work to disfranchise certain citizens.

3. Are you surprised that such laws were not challenged in the courts? Compare these provisions with the guarantees in the Bill of Rights. Do they violate the rights guaranteed in the United States Constitution?

ALAIN LOCKE
The New Negro

Alain Locke has been credited with coining the terms "Harlem Renaissance" and "cultural pluralism," both important concepts during this period. Locke's essay was a significant contribution, but it may be difficult for students to follow. In it Locke announces the goals of the movement and establishes himself as the intellectual leader of the Harlem Renaissance. These goals probably will be clearer to students if they first review the causes and development of the Harlem Renaissance presented in the introduction. Paragraph glossing might help students understand Locke's argument and guide them through his somewhat archaic prose.

To help students focus on the audience, purpose, and specific content of the essay, you can refer them to questions 1, 2, or 3, which draw directly from the reading. Any of these might be used in conjunction with a paragraph-glossing exercise or as the topic of a post-reading small- or large-group discussion.

If your students seem inclined to look at the broader picture, have them respond to question 4, which asks them to relate conditions during the 1920s to those that prevail today. "Contact and cooperation" might be viewed in terms of a microcosm such as the college community. Again, students may want to compare conditions with those portrayed in the civil rights readings in Chapter 6.

♦ Responding

1. Locke explains the movement of blacks from the South to the North "primarily in terms of a new vision of opportunity, of social and economic freedom, of a spirit to seize, even in the face of an extortionate and heavy toll, a chance for the improvement of conditions." Using information from the reading and from your own knowledge, write an essay agreeing or disagreeing with the argument that movement to the North improved conditions for southern blacks in the 1920s.

2. Define what Locke means by the old and new images of the Negro. What diverse elements made up the "largest Negro community in the world" in Harlem in the 1920s?

3. State the purpose of this essay in your own words. Who was Locke's audience? Do you think he was writing primarily for a white or a black audience?

4. Working individually or in a group, list the changes Locke describes as taking place in race relations during the 1920s. Are some of these changes now outdated by other changes in society? Describe the "contact and cooperation" today between diverse groups of people in your community.

ZORA NEAL HURSTON
Sweat

Hurston's lively story should engage students. Part of its appeal is the development of the strong female character Delia. Before students read the selection, they may want to discuss the lack of opportunity for both black and white women during this period; such a discussion may help explain Delia's plight and her actions. A post-reading discussion could focus on question 1, which asks students to look closely at the options available to Delia and compare them to those available today. Question 5 further examines the power relationships between men and women and blacks and whites. Students may wish to discuss the abuse of women.

Another important feature of the story is that it is written in dialect which some students may find difficult to read. A pre-reading discussion of the use of dialect will help make it more accessible. Here is an opportunity for African American students and students from the South to display expertise by reading some examples of the dialect aloud and even explaining some of the rules. Also, it will be enlightening for these students to see their dialect "legitimized" in print.

The class might want to digress into a discussion of writing in dialect. Many students may be unaware that dialect is a legitimate form of a language and that dialects have grammatical and pronunciation rules (Black English is a good example). The development and uses of dialect are possible topics.

Questions 3 and 4 will spark students' imagination by having them write a sequel or a description, respectively.

Other readings that present women who act decisively for good or ill are Cisneros and Ulibarrí (Chapter 7) and Erdrich (Chapter 8).

♦ Responding

1. Working in a group, discuss Delia's predicament and list possible solutions. What community resources might be available today to help her that were not available in the 1920s? Share your ideas with the class.

2. Delia says, "Oh well, whatever goes over the Devil's back, is got to come under his belly. Sometime or ruther, Sykes, like everybody else, is gointer reap his sowing." Summarize the events in the story that illustrate the truth of this proverb.

3. Delia has her revenge at the end of the story, but how will she, a very religious woman, feel the next day? Write a possible sequel to the story in which Delia writes a letter or talks to a trusted friend about her behavior. Alternatively, write an essay discussing the psychological consequences and ethical implications of her actions.

4. Using the comments of the characters in the story, write a physical and psychological description of Sykes.

5. Since the men in the community are aware of Sykes's behavior, why don't they try to help Delia? Discuss whether individuals have a responsibility to try to intervene when they see one person abused by another. Explain Delia's threat to tell the "white folks" and not the black men about Sykes's abuse. What does that choice reveal about power relationships in her community?

LANGSTON HUGHES
Mother to Son; The Negro Speaks of Rivers; Theme for English B

The text deals with the three poems separately, but you may want to treat them as a group. They reflect on the issues of heritage, identity, and ambition and might be discussed in terms of the relationships they depict: mother and child, student and teacher, member and group. Each lends itself to a choral or individual reading, which will illuminate its structure. After the oral reading the class might discuss whether Hughes has incorporated the rhythms of jazz into the poems.

Mother to Son
Question 1 asks students to respond to the mother as the son might. As a pre-writing assignment, students might discuss the son's reaction: Would it be shame, anger, guilt, skepticism? Have students ever had a similar discussion with their parents? Students can use their answers to question 3 to help develop their responses.

   In answering question 2, which asks students to fill in the details of the speaker's life, students might focus on whom she would side with in the controversy over the role of African Americans in the United States: Would it be Booker T. Washington, Marcus Garvey, W. E. B. DuBois? What details of her life experience would cause her to favor one view over another?

   Question 4 is the most challenging, and students may need to discuss racial affirmation before tackling it. Students may not know what conditions African Americans faced when this poem was written. Even the student in "Theme for English B," who has "made it" to some degree, has problems. Students might recall the difficulties of Pardee Lowe (Chapter 2).

♦ Responding

1. Write a letter or poem that the son might write in response to this mother.

2. We don't know many details about the speaker's life. Fill out her character by adding some of the specific facts that you imagine have made her life "no crystal stair."

3. Using your own knowledge and experience, describe some of the problems that the boy might encounter growing up that would make him "set down on the steps."

4. Critics have called this a poem of racial affirmation. Explain why you agree or disagree.

The Negro Speaks of Rivers
Students' reading of this poem probably will be enhanced by some research about the rivers mentioned. If a map or globe is available, locating the rivers will provide a good introduction to the poem.

In discussing question 3, ask students to consider what the span of history covered by the rivers suggests about the "I."

Other works about endurance include Hurston and "Mother to Son" in this chapter, Colón (Chapter 4), and King, Malcolm X, and Farmer (Chapter 6).

♦ Responding

1. With the class, stage a choral reading of the poem for multiple voices. Select parts of the poem to be read by individuals and others to be read by the group. After the reading, discuss the effectiveness of your selections.

2. Discuss Hughes's use of stanza breaks and length of lines to achieve his effects.

3. Identify and discuss the "I" in the poem.

4. Using the campus library, look up all the rivers mentioned in the poem. Share your information with the class. What relation do the rivers have to people of African descent? Write a poem about a place or a part of nature that is particularly important to you.

Theme for English B
Students will relate well to this poem (which refers to Columbia University) because it addresses a familiar situation. They may want to speculate about the autobiographical aspects of the poem. Also, they need to remember that this poem was written when restrictive laws were still on the books in the South and even many northern universities had a quota system for minorities.

Question 3 focuses on the insider/outsider relationship and asks students to apply it to their own experience.

♦ Responding

1. Discuss the ways in which the speaker sees himself as similar to everyone else in his class and the ways in which he sees himself as different.

2. Discuss what the speaker means when he says "you are . . . a part of me, as I am a part of you. That's American." After the discussion, write a prose version of these lines.

3. The speaker is the only "colored" student in his university class. How do you think he feels about that situation? Write about a time when you, a relative, or a friend were the only representative of a group — for example, the only woman or man, the only American, the only northerner — among a group of "others." How did you respond in that situation? How did the others treat you?

JEAN TOOMER
Theater

The same elements that make this story innovative may cause problems for students. A pre-reading discussion may involve reading part of the story aloud and a short discussion of the techniques Toomer uses. A post-reading discussion might begin with analysis of Toomer's purpose in writing the story this way versus a more conventional approach. A summary of the plot (i.e., what did you think was happening in the story, and from whose point of view is the story being told?) would make a good in-class ten-minute writing assignment. This exercise can lead to question 2, which engages students' creativity by asking them to imagine reasons for behavior; question 3 which asks students to relate this situation to one of their own; or question 4, which requires them to write a scene that extends the story. Students might enjoy discussing a "what might occur if" scenario. Often such an exercise allows students to project themselves into the fictional situation and thus reach a greater understanding of the characters.

One problem that may arise when students read this selection is the use of the word *nigger*. Before reading, you might discuss this or review the Beginning exercise in the chapter. After reading, students may want to discuss the second part of question 1, which deals with Toomer's use of *nigger*. Some students may be offended and need to express their feelings; they should be reminded of the context in which this piece was written. This example might be contrasted with the use of *nigger* by white soldiers in the Fauset reading that follows. Students might want to refer again to the Beginning exercise.

♦ Responding

1. Discuss Toomer's use of the word *nigger*. In what ways does its use offend contemporary readers? Do you think it offended readers when the story was written?

2. Working in a group, list the arguments for and against John 's approaching Dorris or the arguments for and against Dorris's approaching John. Combine groups and compare lists.

3. Describe a situation in which you wanted to do something but your anxiety, shyness, or fear of embarrassment kept you from taking risks.

4. Write the scene that might occur if John decided to talk to Dorris. Or describe how John feels afterward about not talking to Dorris.

JESSIE REDMAN FAUSET
There Is Confusion

Although this particular excerpt reveals little about the protagonist, Peter, we chose this reading because it examines the conditions faced by African American soldiers sent to fight in Europe during World War I and deals specifically with the ironies inherent in that situation.

A pre-reading discussion might revolve around the problems writers face when they use fiction as a vehicle for expressing their political points of view. Sometimes the story suffers and its effect on the reader is diminished. As students read, they can evaluate whether this is the case here: Have Fauset's plot and character development suffered because of the political agenda? However, students should realize that this is only one chapter in a complete novel. Question 4, while asking for a personal response, also addresses the realism of the portrayal of the situation and characters. This might tie in with the pre-reading discussion and form the question that begins the follow-up discussion.

You might assign question 1 as a pre-reading question to establish the conditions under which African American soldiers fought. Then you can pool this information and discuss the effects of segregation on black soldiers during World War I. After reading the selection, students can use this background information to answer questions 2 and 3. For question 2, you may need to inform students about Dante's Inferno. For question 3, students might discuss the rationale for segregating the troops and the irony of black soldiers fighting to make the world safe for democracy when blacks in the South were not allowed to vote.

For stories about people who decided not to fight for countries that were denying them rights, see Okada and Yamamoto (Chapter 5).

♦ Responding

1. Using your school library, research the history of segregation within the armed forces. Discuss the practical effects of segregation on black soldiers during World War I.

2. Fauset writes, "Peter thought Dante might well have included this place in the description of his Inferno." Explain why the battlefield was like an image of hell.

3. Discuss the irony of Americans fighting each other when they had been sent to France to fight the Germans. Why do you think the white soldiers were unable to put aside their attitudes toward blacks and concentrate on the war effort?

4. After Peter had numerous intimate talks with the young Quaker physician, "his long bitterness of the years had been assuaged. Henceforth, he told himself, he would try to be more generous in his thoughts of white men." Describe an experience you have had that changed your negative feelings or ideas. Alternatively, discuss whether it is realistic on the author's part to believe that a positive experience with one individual can change attitudes that have been building throughout a lifetime of negative contacts.

WALLACE THURMAN
The Blacker the Berry

This selection, like the Fauset reading, is part of a chapter from a novel, but in this excerpt, the author spends more time letting his readers understand his heroine. It complements the Fauset selection, because one talks about prejudice from without and the other prejudice from within a racial group. This focus, together with a further discussion of the uses of irony, could shape a pre-reading discussion. If time permits, you might show Spike Lee's film *School Daze*. The follow-up discussion could begin with a ten-minute in-class writing assignment asking students to write a scene or a synopsis of what they think will happen next in the story.

Questions 1, 2, and 3 ask students to consider the issue of prejudice within a racial group. This point is especially important because many of the selections in this book deal with the prejudice individuals have endured from members of other ethnic groups. Students can easily visualize minorities as victims of discrimination. While that is, of course, often the case, it is important for them to remember that everyone has prejudices. Sometimes, as in this excerpt, individuals are prejudiced against members of their own racial or ethnic group because of how these people look or behave. You should emphasize that it is not only African Americans who are guilty of such behavior. The class may want to contribute other examples, such as established immigrants who reject new immigrants from their own homelands.

Question 4 hints at the same idea but asks students to use the title of the reading to predict future events.

♦ Responding

1. Emma Lou is a victim of prejudice within her family because she is dark-skinned and female. Yet when she goes to college, she is prejudiced against Hazel Mason because of her behavior. She is aware of her victimization but unaware of her victimizing. In contemporary terms, Emma Lou needs her consciousness raised. Write her a letter making her aware of what she is doing.

2. Working individually or in a group, list all of Hazel Mason's good and bad qualities according to Emma Lou's assessment. From Emma Lou's point of view, consider whether she should befriend her. Do you think the two young women would become friends? Share your reasons with the class.

3. Emma Lou is rejected by the students whom she wishes to befriend. Explain their reasons for rejecting her. This selection illustrates the phenomenon of prejudice within a racial group. Whose criteria are the group members using as their model? Using examples from the selection, your own experience, or sources such as Spike Lee's film *School Daze*, explain the ways in which prejudice within a racial group can distort relationships and undermine the members of the group.

4. Thurman takes the title, *The Blacker the Berry*, from the folk saying "The blacker the berry, the sweeter the juice." Explain why he chose this title and what it reveals about his attitudes toward racial characteristics. Speculate about what he will have Emma Lou come to realize by the end of the novel.

DARWIN TURNER
The Harlem Renaissance: One Facet of an Unturned Kaleidoscope

Turner's article looks at the Harlem Renaissance from a contemporary perspective, as a "serious way of examining the problems of living." Using the image of the kaleidoscope, he asks the reader to look closely at the many themes that emerged during the period. This may be a challenging article for students, and they may need help separating the main points from the examples and following Turner's argument. Paragraph glossing may help them organize the article. Once they understand the content, they might be interested in Turner's comments about selections included in this text (see question 4). Alternatively, you might have a pre-reading discussion about what prompts a majority group to undermine the achievements of a minority group. Since the former already has the power and the numbers, what can it gain from this?

After reading the essay, students can use questions 1, 2, and 3 both to further the discussion begun in the pre-reading and to aid in developing an understanding of Turner's points. These end-of-chapter critical essays have been included to provide both closure and an expanded view of the period and its written products. If you intend to use questions 4 and 5, you may want to bring this up in class. Question 4 asks students to explain Turner's points with fully elaborated examples. Question 5 requires a good understanding of Turner's argument and the ability to use it to counter DuBois and Baraka.

♦ Responding

1. Explain why Turner wants us to twist the kaleidoscope of black life for a different view of the Harlem Renaissance.

2. Contrast the "spectacle" of black failure presented by many white writers of the 1920s with some of the successes Turner mentions. What reasons does he present to explain the distorted picture of blacks in the literature and theater of the time?

3. Working individually or in groups and using examples from the selections in this chapter, illustrate the serious themes dealt with by black writers during the Harlem Renaissance. Discuss the reasons Turner gives to explain why the importance of this work has been obscured.

4. Review Turner's comments about one of the selections in this chapter. Write an essay supporting his statements with fully developed examples from the reading.

5. Write an essay responding to the criticism by W. E. B. DuBois and Imamu Amiri Baraka (LeRoi Jones) that the Harlem Renaissance was "a movement that lost validity as it became a plaything of white culture."

CONNECTING (printed in AMERICAN MOSAIC, p. 239)

Critical Thinking and Writing

For suggestions on how to use these questions see Chapter 1 of this manual. Many of this set ask for comparisons. Questions 2 and 3 ask specifically for comparisons among the readings in this chapter, while 1, 5, 6, 7, 8, and 9 suggest comparisons with other readings in the text. Question 4 requires a general understanding and application of the principles that guided the Harlem Renaissance.

The research questions are broad but can be modified to be used as topics for essays or rephrased into questions that more closely match students' special interests.

CHAPTER 4

PUERTO RICANS: THE VIEW FROM THE MAINLAND

This chapter covers a wider time span than some of the others because the history of Puerto Ricans in the United States is long and varied. The introduction covers the history of Puerto Rico's relationship with the U.S. mainland. It should give students enough background material to allow them to complete the Beginning exercise, which asks them to speculate about the Puerto Ricans' reasons for emigrating. If there are Puerto Rican students in your class, they can lead the discussion.

Beginning: Pre-reading/Writing

In a class discussion, speculate about the political, economic, and personal reasons why Puerto Ricans emigrate to the United States. Consider whether the political relationship between Puerto Rico and the United States creates circumstances for Puerto Ricans that are different from those of immigrants from other countries.

   Following the discussion, students can compare the Puerto Ricans' situation with those of earlier and later immigrants. The early Puerto Rican immigrants arrived at the same time as the big influx of immigrants from Europe. Students might consider how the two groups' situations differed; for example, the Puerto Ricans were American citizens and had been exposed to the English language in Puerto Rico. A question students might want to tackle is whether or not Puerto Rican immigrants have had an easier time than other immigrants.

From The Foraker Act

We included this excerpt from the Foraker Act to point up the limits to Puerto Rican independence that existed at the turn of the century. The act placed Puerto Rico under the jurisdiction of a presidentially appointed military governor and a council with an American majority. It also designated English as the official language. In a pre-reading discussion, you might point out that Puerto Rico was self-governing prior to being ceded to the United States. As the introduction to the

© 1991 Houghton Mifflin Company

chapter points out, the Puerto Rican people had worked hard to win this right from the Spanish Crown.

The responding questions ask students to focus on specifics in the act that indicate the Puerto Ricans' lack of independence. This factor helps explain the early immigrants' interest in politics and makes the Vega essay more understandable.

Question 2 asks students to consider the power structure in Puerto Rico. Is there anything ironic about the United States having this type of power over a territory?

♦ Responding

1. Summarize these provisions of the Foraker Act in your own words. What duties and responsibilities are given to the governor?

2. Consider the way in which officials are chosen to govern Puerto Rico. Who makes these appointments? What role do Puerto Ricans themselves play?

3. How do you think local people reacted to these provisions at the time they were written? Do you think they would react the same way today? Explain any changes in attitude that might have taken place.

BERNARDO VEGA
The customs and traditions of the *tabaqueros* and what it was like to work in a cigar factory in New York City

Vega originally wrote his *Memoirs* in the third person. After he died, his editor, Cesar Andreu Iglesias, transformed the story to a first-person account. We enjoy this reading because it shatters so many stereotypes about blue-collar workers. A pre-reading activity might be to ask students to discuss images of blue-collar workers in the media (for example, "Roseanne") and compare them to blue-collar workers they know personally. Then they can compare those images to the reading and look at question 1, which asks them to focus on stereotypes.

We also like this selection because it presents a working example of student-centered learning. The floor of the cigar factory functions as a classroom, and the workers choose the curriculum. Students should be aware of the workers' focus on social and political issues, the relevance of their reading material, and their commitment to the discussion. A pre-reading activity might focus on the goals of education — especially adult education — and what we might learn from this example.

A post-reading activity might continue this discussion by focusing on questions 2, 3, and 4. If you choose to use question 2 to compare Vega's informal education to the formal one he would have received in a conventional school, you may expand the discussion or introduce an in-class writing assignment to include the Boss's school experience in "A Soul Above Buttons" in Chapter 1. Question 3 retains the focus on the methods and purpose of education, but it leaves room for discussing the Puerto Ricans' interest in politics. You can remind students of the restrictive terms of the Foraker Act and how Puerto Rico had campaigned to gain autonomy from Spain before being ceded to the United States. Vega himself was so committed to political and social issues that he spent his final years working for the proindependence movement in Puerto Rico.

Question 4 can be a very engaging activity. It is more challenging than the other questions because it asks students to use the principles they have learned from the essay to design a modern adult literacy program. This would work well as a group project, and a small- or large-group discussion can serve as pre-writing. The question could be modified to focus on the principles themselves, and isolating them could shape the post-reading discussion.

♦ Responding

1. Think about the image of blue-collar workers that you have formed from your own experience and from the way they have been portrayed in books and in the media. Compare that image to Vega and his fellow *tabaqueros* at the turn of the century. Why did he call them "the most enlightened sector of the working class"? Why were education and political ideas so important to these particular people?

2. Compare the education Vega received in the factory to the formal education he would have received in a traditional school. What are the strengths and weaknesses of each?

3. Vega says, "I remember times when a *tabaquero* would get so worked up defending his position that he didn't mind losing an hour's work — it was piecework — trying to prove his point. He would quote from the books at hand, and if there weren't any in the shop he'd come back the next day with books from home, or from the public library." Why did the workers become so engaged in these issues? Explore the lessons we can learn from this example to promote literacy and improve our educational system.

4. Working individually or in a group, design your own curriculum for an adult literacy class at your local library. Chose readings and discussion topics. Compare your choices with those of the *tabaqueros*.

JESÚS COLÓN
Stowaway; Easy Job, Good Wages; Kipling and I

These three selections come from the book *A Puerto Rican in New York* and recount Colón's experience in coming and adjusting to America. Taken together, these readings look at a number of issues, two of which are the expectations of the new immigrants and the power relationships between the Puerto Ricans and the Americans with whom they had to deal.

A pre-reading activity might deal with the expectations of European immigrants like Panunzio, who arrived during the same period as Colón, and those of the Puerto Ricans. Would they differ, and if so, how? As students read the selections, they can think about whether Colón's expectations were met. Students might enjoy reading the Kipling poem *If* before and after they read the third piece. Students could think about Kipling, his audience, and the advice a father in his world would give his son. What would that son's expectations be? How would they differ from Colón's? Could that poem be relevant to a black Puerto Rican living in New York City in the early 1900s? The irony of the situation should make a good post-reading discussion topic. Question 1 may be helpful in discussing Colón's success or failure in meeting his expectations. Question 5, which deals with the burning of the poem at the end of "Kipling and I," may add depth to the discussion.

The issue of power relationships is another prominent theme in these selections. As pre-reading, it may help students to review the social and political situation at the time the pieces were written. Where would a black Puerto Rican have fit in the power structure of the 1900s? Students can look at the Foraker Act, which defines the power relationships between the United States and Puerto Rico. Alternatively, this discussion may focus on the power structure of the college and even on your own classroom. Question 3 encourages students to discuss this aspect of Colón's work and could be used for a follow-up discussion.

♦ Responding

1. Colón had many problems earning a living in New York City. The cause may have been the economic conditions of the period or Colón's own lack of training and experience. Consider the possibility that he couldn't get a good job because there were no opportunities for Puerto Ricans. Working individually or in a group and using evidence from these selections, list Colón's difficulties and discuss the reasons for them. Share your conclusions with the class.

2. After reading Colón's work, one could argue that he had to confront a system in which material things were more important than human suffering. Write an essay agreeing or disagreeing with this view of American society. You may consider Colón's experience and the historical period he wrote about or deal with the issue in relation to contemporary society.

3. Power relationships seem to play a central role in these three pieces. Those
    who had the ability to hire and fire could set the working conditions. Discuss
    Colón's main objections to the jobs he was able to find. Have you ever been in a
    similar unpleasant situation? Perhaps you were afraid or unable to say
    anything because the person (an employer, a teacher, or a friend) was in a
    position of power. Compare your handling of the situation to Colón's.

4. Imagine that you are the manager of a restaurant. You have just fired Colón
    and he has filed a complaint with the Labor Relations Board. Write a letter to
    the board justifying your action.

5. Why does Colón burn the poem at the end of the third selection? Write an essay
    explaining why a reader might feel that it is a symbolic act as well as an actual
    one.

PIRI THOMAS
Puerto Rican Paradise

This reading focuses on Thomas's mother's nostalgia for Puerto Rico. A pre-reading
activity might involve discussing why the past often seems better than the present.
Students can share stories their parents have told of the "good old days." Questions
1 and 2 can be used to begin follow-up discussions.

Another aspect of the story to explore is the happy family Thomas describes.
Pre-reading questions might include "Do you need money to be happy?" or "What
makes a family happy?" Students could be asked to write for ten minutes about a
particularly happy moment for their families and why it was so satisfying. Another
post-reading discussion might revolve around question 3.

Question 4 brings up a serious controversy: Do you need to be a member of a
group to understand the experience of that group? This discussion might expand to
include questions such as "Who should write about the experiences of minorities?";
"Who should teach ethnic courses or ethnic material?"; "What is the role of the
white teacher and the ethnic student when discussing ethnic material?"; "What is
the importance of books such as this that focus on letting ethnic groups speak for
themselves?" See the poem "Theme for English B" in Chapter 3.

For a different picture of a family experiencing poverty, see Yezierska
(Chapter 1).

♦ Responding

1. How realistic are Thomas's mother's memories of Puerto Rico? Has she
    idealized her childhood? What does Thomas think? He calls the chapter
    "Puerto Rican Paradise." Is that title descriptive or ironic? Using examples

from the reading, describe his mother's life in Puerto Rico and contrast it with the situation in which she finds herself in Harlem.

2. Sometimes when we are unhappy with our present circumstances, we like to think about a time when we were happier. Describe a time when you compared your situation in the present to a happier period in the past. Were your memories accurate, or did you idealize the past? Did your memories help you or hinder you in accepting conditions in the present? What role did such memories play in the Thomas family?

3. The Thomas family had few material comforts, but family members contributed to one another's happiness. Describe the family's activities. How did these compensate or fail to compensate for some of the difficulties of their living conditions? How does your family or the family of someone you know provide financial and emotional support for its members?

4. Mrs. Thomas says, "Only poor people can understand poor people." Does this mean that only by being a member of a group can you understand the experience of someone in that group? Argue for or against this position.

EDWARD RIVERA
Ropes of Passage

This is a complex reading that moves through many scenes: workplace, city, class, and home. The narrator is trying to assert his identity in all of these arenas. One way to approach the reading is to ask students to write for ten minutes about a time when they were in a frustrating situation at home, in school, or on the streets. Then students can read their work aloud and discuss how they responded to the situations. This assignment may help them understand the pressures Santos encountered that kept him from insisting on the correct change, finishing his exam, or moving out on his own.

Questions 1 and 3 may be interesting follow-ups to this approach. An alternative is to focus on the process of developing an identity. Students could begin by discussing, in small or large groups, how much control they think they have in deciding who they are. They might recall times when they made a conscious decision to change something about themselves either to fit in or to make themselves stand out.

Question 2 could serve as a post-reading activity. However, students should be familiar with Santos's reading materials before attempting this question.

See Villarreal in Chapter 7 for another reading that deals with the impact of education on an immigrant family.

♦ Responding

1. Santos is a victim of an injustice when he receives the wrong change at the
    bookstore. Discuss his response. Why doesn't he fight harder for his rights?
    Why doesn't the floorwalker believe him? What would your reaction be in a
    similar situation?

2. Santos criticizes the payroll manager's addiction to elegant language and
    British spelling and his art teacher's use of "old boy." These characters are
    appropriating elements of a culture that is not their own in order to impress
    others. Could they argue that Santos, too, is appropriating elements of a
    culture that is not his own in order to impress others? Could they argue that
    Santos, too, is appropriating an identity that is not his own? Examine Santos's
    reading material and dreams, and argue for or against this point of view.

3. Santos is unable or unwilling to write his "sociological autobiography" for the
    test. Consider how he might answer the question and write the answer for him,
    choosing incidents from the reading to illustrate how society's beliefs and
    attitudes influence his life.

4. Santos says, "During that time I decided to move out. The Elysian Arms
    escapade hadn't been just an impulse after all. But back in bed, nearly asleep,
    I knew I wasn't going anywhere just yet, maybe never." Working in two groups,
    list the factors that keep Santos at home and the reasons why he wants to
    move out, or list the pros and cons of his staying at home and moving out. After
    comparing the lists, write an essay describing what you think Santos will be
    doing in ten years.

NICHOLASA MOHR
A Thanksgiving Celebration

You might begin your discussion by considering why Mohr chose Thanksgiving as
the focus of her story. One approach is to contrast the situation of the Pilgrims,
who had the Native Americans to be thankful for, with that of the new
immigrants. Who welcomes them, and for whom should they be thankful? For
whom should Amy be thankful?

This story is one of several in the book that show women coping despite difficult
circumstances. Others are Hurston's "Sweat" (Chapter 3) and Ulibarrí's "My
Grandma Smoked Cigars" and Cisneros' "Woman Hollering Creek" (Chapter 7).
These contrast with some of the works that portray women as victims, such as
Yezierska's "Fat of the Land" and Rolvaag's "Facing the Great Desolation"
(Chapter 1) and Mora's "Illegal Alien" (Chapter 7).

A possible pre-reading activity is to discuss portrayals of women. The discussion could begin with the readings the class has covered and move on to other books and the media. It would be interesting to hear students' expectations about how female characters will behave when they encounter problems. This story puts the heroine in a difficult situation, but she copes with it well and solves her problems in a creative way. The question "Does the time in which a piece is written and the sex of the author have any impact on the portrayal of women?" might begin a post-reading discussion.

Question 3 asks students to discuss the importance of family stories, a significant theme throughout the text. Having students think about the role stories have played in their own families will allow them to recognize the stories' significance and perhaps encourage them to record and preserve some of their own.

Question 4 focuses on the readers' expectations and asks them to write an alternative ending to the story. Students may prefer a tragic ending. This question aims to get them to think about other possibilities and to analyze their responses both to the story as it is written and to other versions. All of this can tie into the issue of the portrayal of women and even be an alternative organizing principle for the course.

♦ Responding

1. Amy says to herself, "If I make it through this day . . . I'll be all right." Explain why this Thanksgiving is so important to her.

2. Amy lies to her children about the eggs. What is the reason for the lie? If she had asked your advice, what would you have advised her to tell her children?

3. The family stories represent more than just pleasant memories. Discuss their importance to Amy. Why does she choose this time to tell them to her children? What is the role of stories in your family? Share a family story that is important to you.

4. At the beginning of the story we learn that Amy, a widow with four children, is living on welfare in a rundown apartment in a poor neighborhood. Given this situation, explain why you might have expected an optimistic or a pessimistic resolution. Mohr chooses an optimistic ending. What do you think she is saying about Amy? Write an alternate ending for the story, and compare it with Mohr's.

JUDITH ORTIZ COFER
The Line of the Sun

Marisol, like Piri Thomas's mother, idealizes life in Puerto Rico. A possible pre-
reading question is to have students imagine what their lives might have been like
had they been born in a different time and place. They could also question why
someone would want to change the time or place of his or her birth. Marisol, like
many of the other characters in this text (and like many of our students), is caught
"halfway between cultures." This can be a very uncomfortable position, and its
difficulties should be discussed either before or after reading the selection.

Question 1 focuses on the bicultural issue. Students may not understand or
sympathize with Marisol's dissatisfaction with life in the United States. If this is
the case, use question 2 to call on students to look back at the text and speculate.
As this question suggests, Marisol uses visions of Puerto Rico to escape from
current problems. Students might discuss the effectiveness of this strategy and
relate it to their own behavior.

Questions 3 and 4 discuss Marisol's relationship with her mother. Some
students may share the problems of wanting to fit in when you are an outsider
(Marisol's views of herself in school) and embarrassment about immigrant parents.
Others may not understand why it bothers Marisol to have a mother who is
"exotic." A discussion of her attitudes could bring up these different points of view.
A ten-minute writing assignment about whether students feel Marisol's reaction to
her mother's visit to school was appropriate or mature could precede the
discussion.

◆ Responding

1. Marisol describes herself as "halfway between cultures." Compare her lifestyle
    at fifteen in Paterson, New Jersey, with what her life would have been like if
    she had been born and raised in Puerto Rico.

2. Describe Puerto Rico as Marisol pictures it. In what ways do you think she
    might idealize the Island? Discuss the role of Puerto Rico in helping her deal
    with her everyday life. Is there a place or a person you think about when you
    want to escape from current problems?

3. Discuss Marisol's reaction to her mother's visit to her school. What image does
    she have in mind for her ideal mother? Describe a time when you or someone
    you know was in a situation where you felt out of place and wanted to fit in.

5. Working individually or in a group, discuss the conflict of wills between mother
    and daughter. List examples of their encounters and the reaction of each. How
    much of Marisol's behavior do you think is adolescent rebellion, and how much
    is a response to her mother's personality?

JUAN FLORES
Puerto Rican Literature in the United States: Stages and Perspectives

Flores provides a rich survey of literature by Puerto Ricans living in the United States. Like the Turner essay in Chapter 3, this piece places some of the writers in this chapter in a broader context. Students should enjoy reading Flores's analysis. As an in-class post-reading assignment, students might use the information from the essay to construct a chart showing the stages in the emergence of Puerto Rican literature.

Flores brings up issues that are central to the creation of texts of this type. Questions 1 and 2, on the literary canon, ask students to consider the validity of multicultural texts and, by extension, multicultural curricula. Such a question might frame the entire course. Some related issues students might discuss is the inclusion of ethnic literature and history at all grade levels. Minority students in our classes often have expressed resentment over the fact that they spend so much of their education studying the culture and history of the majority while so little attention is paid to theirs. This may provoke some disagreement from majority students. You might want to ask them to discuss their feelings about studying minority literature.

Questions 3 and 4 are text specific. If students make up the chart, they can use it to construct the outline required in question 3.

♦ Responding

1. Working individually or in a group, define "literary canon." What works are traditionally part of the American literary canon? What does Flores want to include?

2. Using examples from the readings as well as your own experience, argue for or against broadening the canon. For additional information, you might want to read the essay by David Mura in Chapter 9.

3. Outline the stages in the development of Puerto Rican literature that Flores defines in his article.

4. According to Flores, what are the characteristics of immigrant literature? Compare immigrant literature to what Flores calls "minority literature." How is contemporary Puerto Rican literature distinct from both? Write an essay agreeing or disagreeing with Flores when he says that Puerto Rican literature is "a literature operative within and between two national literatures and marginal in both. . . . This inclusion within, or integral association with, a different and in some ways opposing national culture stretches the notion of a pluralist American canon to the limit."

CONNECTING (printed in AMERICAN MOSAIC, p. 318)

Critical Thinking and Writing

Like the other sets of connecting questions, these attempt to help students see the parallels between the experiences of one writer and another, one group and another. Questions 1 and 5 specifically ask students to support their points with examples from within this chapter. Questions 2, 6, and 7 point up relationships across chapters.

The remaining questions are more general. Students are always encouraged to use specific examples, but their choices can come from other sources as well as their own experience. However, the research questions require information from outside sources. For additional suggestions about ways to use the questions, see the remarks in Chapter 1 of this manual.

CHAPTER 5

JAPANESE AMERICANS: THE INTERNMENT EXPERIENCE

This chapter centers around the experience of Japanese Americans during their internment by the United States government in World War II. Although the Japanese have a long history in the United States, we chose to focus on the internment period for two reasons. First, we believe that Japanese Americans suffered a terrible wrong when they were interned. Second, the internment experience for Japanese Americans, like the Holocaust for many European Jews, generated a great deal of eloquent writing. All the readings in this chapter deal with this important but little known period in American history.

Beginning: Pre-reading/Writing

Imagine yourself in the following situation: A government agency has informed you that you must leave your home in seven days and go to an internment camp. You can take only two small suitcases and a bag of bedding with you. How do you react to what is happening? What will you do? What will you take with you and why? Share your choices with the class.

You might use the Beginning exercise before students read the introduction. It asks students to imagine themselves in the situation that many Japanese and Japanese Americans on the West Coast faced. These groups were suddenly and inexplicably ordered to leave their homes. If students question this order, you might answer that during this period the immigrants had to leave simply because the law ordered them to do so. Part of the follow-up discussion could address the bewilderment these people undoubtedly felt. Students might also want to talk about what they would most regret leaving behind. This exercise should help students to empathize with the Japanese and Japanese Americans when they read the introduction.

Japanese Relocation Order

This executive order gave the secretary of war the power to evacuate from specific military areas any residents who were considered risks to national security. Legal documents typically are dense, and sometimes their implications are ambiguous. In this case, no specific ethnic group was mentioned, yet the order was applied almost exclusively to Japanese Americans. You might ask students how they would account for that: Is that provision in the document itself? After reading the order, you may want to ask students to look at questions 1, 2, and 3 which require them to carefully reread the order. They might compare the document to the Exclusion Act (Chapter 2) or to the "grandfather clauses" in some southern states' constitutions that disfranchised African Americans (Chapter 3). This can open a discussion on lawmakers' manipulation of words to disguise their true purpose. It can also call into question the ability of the Bill of Rights (Chapter 1) and the Constitution to protect citizens' rights.

Question 4 asks students to analyze the order's impact on citizens' civil rights. This issue requires much thought, and is a theme that recurs throughout this chapter. Students might want to read further before tackling this question in writing. During post-reading discussion, try to get them to think about whether and under what conditions such an invasion of citizens' rights could occur again.

♦ Responding

1. Explain the government's reasons for issuing this order.

2. How did the act directly or indirectly indicate that the Japanese would be forced to live in relocation centers?

3. Identify the powers given to the "appropriate military commander."

4. This order has been called "the most drastic invasion of the rights of citizens of the U.S. by their own government that has thus far occurred in the history of our nation" (E. S. Corwin). Explain this statement. Do you agree or disagree with it? Support your answer.

MONICA SONE
Pearl Harbor Echoes in Seattle

Sone's autobiography is a good place to begin reading, because she recounts some of the legal and historical background presented in the introduction. Further, her story depicts the effects of the Relocation Order on a real family. The introduction to the chapter and the Relocation Order can serve as pre-reading for this selection. The excerpt from *Farewell to Manzanar* that follows provides a natural sequel, so these two selections might be read together.

After seeing the practical effects of the Relocation Order, students may be better prepared to answer question 1, which is another version of question 4 in the preceding section. This is an important issue and should be dealt with at some point in this chapter.

By asking students to use a letter format, question 2 will force students to visualize an audience other than the instructor and help them learn to write for different audiences and purposes.

Questions 3 or 4 could be used to structure post-reading activities. The resulting outline or list of attitudes could be the topic of a whole-class discussion. For question 4, students could also compare these attitudes and reactions of a real family with the stereotype from which the government allegedly was protecting itself.

◆ Responding

1. Sone states that the internment of her family violated their rights as American citizens. Using examples from her autobiography and from other readings, such as the Bill of Rights, write an essay agreeing or disagreeing with her statement.

2. Have you ever felt that your rights were taken away unfairly by a social institution, family, or friend? Write a letter of protest to the individual or institution who you felt treated you unjustly.

3. Working individually or in a group, outline the changes that took place in the lives of the Sone family between the bombing of Pearl Harbor and the evacuation of the Japanese Americans.

4. Compare the attitudes and reactions of different members of the family toward the United States and Japan before and after Pearl Harbor, or before and after the evacuation order. Did the older generation have a markedly different attitude from that of the younger generation?

JEANNE WAKATSUKI HOUSTON AND JAMES HOUSTON
From Farewell to Manzanar

The Houston selection follows Sone because it takes the reader directly into a camp like the one in which the Sone family was interned. Houston describes the camp from a child's perspective. As a pre-reading activity, you might ask students some of the following questions: What do you imagine the camps were like? What do you think the internees would most miss? Students can use information from the introduction and their own knowledge to visualize life in the camps. Their speculations can then be checked against the description of the camp in the reading.

Questions 1, 2, and 3 could serve as the basis for small-group or whole-class post-reading discussions. You might ask students to draw a picture of the camp and then share their drawings with the class. You can focus on what each student chose to draw and why that image was especially significant to him or her. You might want to take question 3 further and ask students what methods they would use for coping.

Question 4 brings up another aspect of the internment, the attitudes of the internees toward America. As either a pre- or post-reading activity, students can discuss what might motivate the different reactions and even what they think their own reactions might have been. This is a good time to mention the many Japanese Americans who volunteered to serve in the armed forces. However, you also should acknowledge that some Japanese Americans' loyalty shifted to Japan, as the next three selections describe. Where do students think the Sone family's loyalties would lie?

♦ Responding

1. Describe or draw a picture of the camp at Manzanar. Share your work with the class.

2. Working individually or in a group, list the hardships of camp life. What would you find most intolerable?

3. Houston talks about "the turning of our life in camp, from the outrageous to the tolerable. . . . You try to re-create, as well as you can, your normality, some sense of things continuing." Discuss the strategies that people interned at Manzanar used to cope with their situation and make it bearable.

4. Houston writes, "The fact that America had accused us, or excluded us, or imprisoned us, or whatever it might be called, did not change the kind of world we wanted. Most of us were born in this country; we had no other models." Using evidence from the story, analyze the attitude of the internees at Manzanar toward America and American ideas.

TOSHIO MORI
Unfinished Message

Mori's story describes the experience of Japanese Americans who enlisted in the American army. The irony of their position and that of their families is particularly significant. Japanese American units were among those most highly decorated for bravery, yet their families were interned during this period. The mother in the story is still living in a relocation camp and needs a travel permit to visit her wounded son. A pre-reading exercise might ask students to explore what motivated the Japanese American soldiers to defend the same country that had imprisoned their families. How could their loyalty have been questioned?

Question 1 focuses on the irony of the Japanese American soldiers' situation. To point up the irony, you can have students read Mirikitani's "Desert Flowers."

Question 2 concerns the fighting record of the Japanese American soldiers. Collins's *Native American Aliens*, listed in the reference section of this chapter, is one source for statistics on the Japanese American units.

Question 3 deals with supernatural aspects of the story that students may find compelling.

Question 4 could be the topic of an in-class 30-minute writing assignment. Scenes could be read aloud or circulated and read silently.

♦ Responding

1. Kazuo is a soldier fighting for the United States in World War II. Why does his mother need a travel permit to visit him? What justification might the government give for such restrictions? How might the Japanese American soldier respond? Discuss your own possible reaction to this situation.

2. Research the fighting record of Japanese American soldiers in World War II.

3. Do you believe that Kazuo's mother knew her son was in danger? Did she try to communicate with him from beyond the grave? What do you think the author believes? Present evidence from the text to support your opinion.

4. The author doesn't report the scene that takes place between the mother and the wounded son when they meet. Write your own version of that meeting.

JOHN OKADA
From No-No Boy

This excerpt from the novel tells the story of a Japanese American who refused to enlist in the U.S. army and at war's end must face others who made different choices. His situation is further complicated by the attitude of his mother and his own dilemma of being torn between two loyalties and two identities. As a pre-reading discussion, students could consider his situation and describe what they think they would do if they were caught in this bind. Alternatively, students could be asked how they determine their loyalties.

Question 1 deals with the issue of dual identity, a theme that recurs throughout this book (see Mora in Chapter 7). Many students may have experienced conflicts between their native cultures and mainstream American culture. We often see students whose loyalty to their language and culture make even learning English an act of betrayal. For them, going to college can mean turning their backs on families who don't understand their ambitions or the changes they have undergone. Question 3 allows such students to discuss their personal resolution of this problem.

Question 2 could be used as a ten-minute in-class writing assignment designed to begin discussion of the story. Question 4 might serve as the basis for a small-group or whole-class post-reading discussion.

♦ Responding

1. Ichiro's statement "I wish with all my heart that I were Japanese or that I were American" expresses his inner conflict. Explain the loyalties that pull him in different directions.

2. What is Ichiro's attitude toward his mother? Does it change in the course of the story? If you were Ichiro, what would you say to your mother on the way home from the Kumasakas'?

3. Have you ever found yourself in serious conflict over a matter of conscience with a person whose opinion you value, such as a parent, teacher, religious leader, or special friend? Did the conflict produce inner turmoil? What was the outcome?

4. The story presents two contrasting attitudes toward Japan and America. Compare these viewpoints and present the reasons for each.

HISAYE YAMAMOTO
Las Vegas Charley

This story views the internment experience from the perspective of an immigrant from Japan. This broader framework allows the reader to follow the main character from his early years in Japan to the end of his life in the United States. His story depicts the history of many Japanese immigrants who came to America and subsequently lost much of their cultural identity.

A pre-reading question might ask students to consider why this story is called "Las Vegas Charley." This could lead to a longer discussion about the significance of names. Students who have anglicized their names may want to explain why they did so and how they feel about the change. Some may prefer American names because they are easier for strangers to pronounce and provide the new immigrants with a sense of belonging. Others may have retained their original names or wish they had. Still others may have names they use with family and close friends and others that they use in school.

Question 1 directly confronts the issue of names and asks students to consider "Charley" from the author's perspective. You can tie this discussion into the problem of dual identity that has plagued many of the writers in this book.

Question 2 would work for a small-group or whole-class post-reading discussion. Question 3, which asks whether Charley was a victim of fate, would make a suitable ten-minute in-class writing assignment.

For another reading that explores choice versus circumstance, see Lowe (Chapter 2).

♦ Responding

1. The narrator introduces the main character as "the old Japanese that everyone knew as Charley (he did not mind being called that — it was as good a name as any and certainly easier to pronounce . . .)." Do you think that Yamamoto would agree that the name change is unimportant? Discuss the relationship between a name and a person's sense of identity.

2. Working individually or in a group, summarize the main events of Charley's life. Using information from the introduction and other sources, discuss which of Charley's experiences represented the experiences of many Japanese immigrants and which were the result of his character.

3. Was Charley a victim of fate? What choices were made for him? What choices did he make?

4. What did Noriyuki finally understand about his father?

JANICE MIRIKITANI
We, the Dangerous; Desert Flowers; For My Father

These three poems view the internment years from the perspective of the present. They demonstrate how artists can use collective experiences to create works of art and literature. They also reflect the lingering effect of the internment period on Japanese Americans. Mirikitani herself was born in 1942 and probably wouldn't have any conscious memory of the internment; yet it is the theme of these poems.

The questions are designed to help students see that the horrors of the internment have been repeated and that stereotypical portraits of minority groups lead others to see them as less than human. Some of the questions give students the opportunity to examine their own pasts and use them as the basis for creative expression.

In question 2 for "We, the Dangerous," students can contrast the characteristics of Japanese Americans presented with those of families in any of the other readings.

Choral readings of one or all of the poems will enhance the poems' drama. Let students organize the readings and assign the parts. Then, as a post-reading activity, they can discuss the reasons for their choices and try out other options.

♦ Responding

We, the Dangerous

1. Plan a class choral reading of this poem. How would you divide it for different voices? Explain your reasons. What does the reading reveal about the differences between the "I," "we," and "they" of the poem?

2. Through whose eyes do we see the characteristics of "We, the Dangerous"? Would the poet agree that these are the characteristics of Japanese Americans, or does she believe that they are stereotypes about Asians common during World War II?

3. Compare the effects of the opening and closing stanzas of the poem. How do you respond to the repetition of words and phrases? If you had to assign an emotion to the voice used by the poet, what would it be?

4. What is the relationship between Hiroshima, Vietnam, and Tule Lake? Why does the author include Hiroshima and Vietnam in a poem about the internment experience? From the evidence in the poem, who do you think the author believes is really dangerous?

Desert Flowers

1. Discuss the irony of Japanese Americans in internment camps making flowers for the American Legion.

2. In the second stanza, line 11, "That" is capitalized, but "america" in line 31 and in stanza 3, line 5, is not. Discuss possible reasons why the poet has defied conventional capitalization rules and what she may be trying to convey by doing so.

3. Mirikitani writes about her past. Write your own poem about a past event in your family or your culture that still influences your attitudes and behavior.

For My Father

1. Mirikitani draws a verbal picture of her father's character and the events that shaped it. Working individually or in a group, use the clues from the poem to write a prose description of this man.

2. Discuss the attitude of the speaker toward her father. Use examples from the poem to support your points.

3. Write a poem or an essay that captures the essence of someone important to you.

RONALD TAKAKI
Roots

This reading also views the internment experience from today's perspective. Takaki encourages Japanese Americans to join him in breaking their silence about their experience. This silence, which reflects the traditional Japanese way of coping with hardship, might have barred them from finding release from the shame and guilt produced by the internment. A pre-reading discussion might focus on the victims' feelings of guilt and ask students to speculate about the attitudes of Japanese Americans today: Have they forgotten the internment? If not, do they tell their children and grandchildren about it? Why did it take so long for the United States government to make reparations?

To answer question 1, students may need to gather more information about Japanese culture. Japanese or Japanese American students or your school's Asian language and literature department would be good resources. Students can make some inferences from the introduction and the other readings in the chapter.

Question 3 asks students to again consider names commonly applied to ethnic groups. You might relate this discussion to the material on names in Chapter 3. Students often are unaware that the term *Oriental* is pejorative. An open discussion about the use of names and sensitivity to the feelings of ethnic group members would be appropriate here. You might begin by asking students if anyone has ever called them names and how they felt when that happened. Then they can discuss appropriate reactions. If the class is uncomfortable with controversial issues, you might ask them to consider the effect on children of being called names; that will distance the discussion and perhaps make it more comfortable.

Question 4 ties in well with the Mura reading in Chapter 9.

♦ Responding

1. Explain why Congressman Norman Mineta said that ex-internees have been " 'stigmatized'. . . carrying the 'burden of shame' for over forty painful years."

What did the Japanese Americans feel ashamed about? Using information from the readings and your own knowledge of human nature, discuss the fact that though they were the victims of an injustice, they felt shame rather than anger. Does Japanese culture help explain this reaction, or are feelings of shame and guilt typical reactions of victims?

2. What caused Japanese Americans finally to break their silence about the internment? Discuss the role of their stories in helping the younger generation understand themselves and their heritage.

3. Thinking about the connotations of names of ethnic groups, explain the role of names in forming group images and individual identities. Consider the effect on children of derogatory names.

4. Read David Mura's "Strangers in the Village" (Chapter 9). Compare his attitudes toward the history and literature studied in most American schools with the attitudes expressed by the young Asian Americans in this reading.

CONNECTING (printed in AMERICAN MOSAIC, p. 395)

Critical Thinking and Writing

You might choose questions 1 and 10 of this set as the basis for discussion, debate, or formal papers after students have read the entire chapter. These topics deal with two central issues of this chapter: motivation for the internment and reparations. Although students should have enough information for discussion after reading this chapter, you might want to suggest some outside research to supplement the information provided in the text.

The other questions vary in focus. Questions 2, 3, 4, and 8 point up specific connections to other parts of the text. Questions 5, 6, and 9 ask students to use material from the text to support their points about broad issues. Question 7 asks for a personal response.

The research questions in this section ask for specific answers. Students might want to work on scaled down versions of these questions. Alternatively, you could introduce them as in-class discussion topics.

CHAPTER 6

AFRICAN AMERICANS: THE STRUGGLE FOR CIVIL RIGHTS

The civil rights period is an important era in recent American history. During that time, many Americans joined to support the ideal of racial equality. Issues such as the prevalence of racism and the lack of equal opportunity emerged and persist today. The case *Brown* v. *The Board of Education*, the Montgomery bus boycott, the sit-ins, and the Freedom Riders led to legislation such as the Voting Rights Act of 1965 and effected profound changes in society. Schools and public facilities were desegregated, and the public at large was made aware of the brutality of racism. These events are recent enough for students to have discussed them with family members who participated firsthand. Students might begin this chapter by pooling their own knowledge about the civil rights movement: How important was it? Did it change the circumstances of their lives? Students who have no knowledge about this period could interview relatives and older friends about their recollections.

The introduction to the chapter reviews the historical context and summarizes events. For a more dramatic introduction to the period, you might show the first episode of the PBS series "Eyes on the Prize."

Beginning: Pre-reading/Writing

Before reading the selections in this chapter, try to determine how much you actually know about the civil rights movement and its leaders by listing events that led up to and took place during the struggle for civil rights. Working with the class, construct a timeline of significant events. As you read the selections and learn more about the civil rights movement, revise your timeline as necessary.

Students can use information from the introduction to the chapter and their interviews with relatives and friends to construct the timeline.

From Brown v. The Board of Education of Topeka

Students should be made aware that this was a landmark decision and that it paved the way for many other changes. By including this document, we hoped to call attention to the issue of segregation of schools, lunch counters, restrooms, and other public places. As a pre-reading activity, you might ask students to imagine themselves in a situation where they were restricted from certain areas of the campus because of some physical characteristic such as the color of their eyes or hair. How would they feel? How would they behave? How would the quality of their education change?

An alternative pre-reading activity could focus on helping students understand the importance of the *Brown* decision. You might introduce the *Plessy* v. *Ferguson* (1896) decision, which permitted "separate but equal" schools. Students could discuss what the principle of "separate but equal" meant in practice. Question 3 could serve as a post-reading activity.

A copy of the Fourteenth Amendment would enhance the post-reading discussion. This can lead to a discussion about how access to education can be viewed as protection.

Questions 2 and 4 provide follow-up topics for papers or discussion.

♦ Responding

1. Explain the significance of the Fourteenth Amendment to the Constitution.

2. List the reasons that the justices give to support their statement "Today, education is perhaps the most important function of state and local governments." Which of these reasons do you think is most persuasive and important? Write an essay supporting your choice.

3. Working individually or in a group, define *segregation*, *de facto segregation*, and *separate but equal*. Discuss the ways in which these policies were implemented in many school systems.

4. Using arguments from the decision as well as from your own knowledge and experience, agree or disagree that "in the field of public education the doctrine of 'separate but equal' has no place. " Consider whether the same arguments apply to private education.

RALPH ELLISON
From Invisible Man

This reading predates the civil rights period having been written two years before *Brown* v. *The Board of Education* and ten years before the freedom rides, but we included it for several reasons. Ellison is an important writer, and the reading points up some of the difficulties African Americans faced both in the South and in the North. It also highlights the convictions and emotions that led to the civil rights movement.

A pre-reading discussion might focus on the problems of African Americans in the North. Some students might be very knowledgeable about the situation; for others you may need to provide additional information. You can suggest that they draw conclusions from the readings in Chapter 3: What expectations might an African American coming from the South during the period of the Harlem Renaissance have had about life in the North? Students might also speculate about the feelings of the soldiers coming back from World War II.

Questions 1, 2, and 4 would all serve to focus post-reading discussions. Each establishes how the mounting feelings of dispossession could have resulted in the actions described in the excerpt and ultimately throughout the nation. Students may want to look closely at the language and note how often the words *ashamed*, *embarrassed*, and *fear* appear in the story before the narrator takes action.

If students work on question 2, they might want to follow up with a discussion of question 7 in the Connecting section, which asks them to compare this excerpt to Spike Lee's film *Do the Right Thing* in terms of the causes of the escalating conflict. What was the "right thing" for the tenants, the crowd, and the marshalls to do in this situation?

Question 3 asks students to look closely at the tone and techniques of persuasion used in both speeches. If students have difficulty seeing the parallels, you might have them examine Marc Antony's speech for evidence of irony, repetition of key phrases, and other rhetorical strategies. Then you could have them work in groups to locate examples of these techniques in Ellison's piece. Students can list the techniques and use them to analyze Martin Luther King, Jr.'s letter and speech, presented later in the chapter.

♦ Responding

1. The narrator in this selection says, "It was as though I myself was being dispossessed of some painful yet precious thing which I could not bear to lose." In an essay, explain why the narrator identifies with the couple being evicted and why he feels dispossessed.

2. Working individually or in a group, examine the events in this narrative chronologically and explain how each subsequent event escalates hostilities. Identify the interchanges that particularly move the onlookers to anger.

3. Compare the narrator's speech to the crowd to Marc Antony's speech to the crowd in Shakespeare's play *Julius Caesar*. What techniques do both speakers use to move people to action?

4. How do the narrator's feelings about his identity change during the course of this incident?

JAMES FARMER
"Tomorrow Is for Our Martyrs"

Farmer was an important leader in the fight for civil rights, but he may be unfamiliar to students. Have them review CORE to appreciate its importance.

This selection from Farmer's autobiography discusses the murder of three civil rights workers who went to Mississippi to initiate a large-scale voter registration drive among African Americans. This movement met with resistance from local communities. The reading presents some of the complexities of the civil rights period as well as some of the dangers civil rights activists faced.

Your students may have trouble comprehending the extent of the racism and community-supported violence in the United States. Some students already know about these events or learned about them from the film *Mississippi Burning*. If not, you could show the film before students read the selection to set the scene. This could also help students recognize the danger to the three men and the fear and hostility that prevailed in the white communities. However, you should point out that the film was criticized because it elevated the role of the white FBI agents at the expense of the blacks' role. Following the reading, the class could compare the version of events in Farmer's piece with that in the film.

Questions 1, 2, and 3 provide topics for post-reading discussions. Question 1 may require some background on the nonviolent approach advocated by King; students could read "Letter from a Birmingham Jail" at this time.

If you want to focus on the complexities of the period, you can review the political situation. What was at stake for whites if more blacks were able to vote and generally were integrated into the community? What was at stake for blacks if the power base changed? Have students refer to the introduction to the chapter and to other sources to fill in the context.

You might ask students what would inspire members of the power group to assist the oppressed and vice versa. If you choose this approach, questions 3, 4, and 5 can focus the discussion and serve as writing topics.

Question 2 raises an important issue and is a possible topic for in-class writing or discussion followed by a formal paper. Questions 3 and 4 offer topics for follow-up discussion.

♦ Responding

1. Describe the circumstances in which Farmer says, "I was not Christ. I was not Gandhi. I was not King." Why was it especially hard for him to practice nonviolence at that moment? Using your own knowledge, speculate about what arguments Christ, Gandhi, or King might present for turning the other cheek.

2. Using examples from the reading or from your own experience, write an essay explaining the phrase "Evil societies always kill their consciences."

3. Members of the African American community possessed information about the

murder of Chaney, Schwerner, and Goodman but didn't come forward immediately. Working in a group, discuss why having such information would be dangerous. What difficulties would African Americans have in getting the information to someone they could trust?

4. Farmer implies that the three civil rights workers were "fingered" by an African American. What might explain such a betrayal? Why might some members of the African American community cooperate with a Caucasian sheriff?

5. Members of CORE and other groups — both African American and Caucasian — who went to the South to register voters willingly risked their lives. Does such idealism exist in America today? Support your position using examples from the readings, current events, or personal feelings and experiences.

MARTIN LUTHER KING, JR.
Letter from Birmingham Jail; I Have a Dream

These pieces are classics, and students may have read them previously. Students can gain fresh insights, however, by reading them within the context of the other readings in this chapter and the text. We included them because they so sharply define King's position on nonviolence and the writing is so persuasive and moving.

Letter from Birmingham Jail
The author's note at the beginning of this reading helps set the context. If you would like to focus on King's purpose in writing the letter, you can have students speculate, using the introduction or their own knowledge, on what the clergymen wrote about King's activities to elicit such a lengthy response. As students read, have them pay special attention to the issues King brings up and how he defends his activities and persuades his readers to join him.

An understanding of King's position on nonviolence is essential to an appreciation of the civil rights period. If you choose to explore this philosophy, you can discuss the general concept of "turning the other cheek" and what can be gained from such an approach as a pre-reading activity. You can have students take their own stand on nonviolence before reading the selection and see where they agree or disagree with King following the reading. Students could also compare King's view of the nonviolence question with that of Malcolm X, whose position is presented in the next selection. If students saw *Do the Right Thing,* you might point out that Lee ends the film with quotations from both King and Malcolm X regarding violence as a solution to problems. Why did he choose quotations that express opposing points of view?

Still another approach is to look at the ironies of the situation depicted in the reading. Using their knowledge about the period gained from the introduction to this chapter and other selections, students could assemble lists of crimes committed by whites against blacks during this time — murder, destruction of property, obstructing the right to vote, and so forth. In some cases, even the clergy was involved as depicted in the Farmer piece. This background should help students put King's crime of parading without a license into perspective. They may also want to address the question of whether King was merely exercising his right of freedom to assemble. Questions 2 and 3 can then be used to focus the post-reading discussion.

As an alternate post-reading activity, students can use questions 1 and 2 to evaluate the success of King's arguments.

♦ Responding

1. Write an essay agreeing or disagreeing with the following statement: "Injustice anywhere is a threat to justice everywhere. We are caught in an inescapable network of mutuality, tied in a single garment of destiny. Whatever affects one directly, affects all indirectly."

2. Argue for or against the following proposition: ". . . an individual who breaks a law that conscience tells him is unjust, and who willingly accepts the penalty of imprisonment in order to arouse the conscience of the community over its injustice, is in reality expressing the highest respect for law."

3. Working individually or in a group, discuss the reasons that Dr. King was in jail when he was fighting injustice.

4. In your opinion, has the hope that Dr. King expresses in the last paragraph of the letter been realized? Support your position with examples from your reading, experience, or television news reports or special programs.

I Have a Dream
We recommend that you try to get a video of King's speech. His delivery highlights the structure of the speech and allows the audience to experience the full impact of his style. African American and other students may be familiar with the style of preachers in black churches and be able to comment on the style. Be careful, however, that discussion of King's style does not obscure his message.

Questions 2 and 3 for "I Have a Dream" present activities that highlight the techniques of speech writing and delivery.

♦ Responding

1. Working individually or in a group, locate the parts of the speech in which King gives advice to his followers. Summarize that advice and discuss how it exemplifies his philosophy of nonviolent resistance to injustice.

2. Working with the rest of the class, develop a list of criteria for effective political speeches. Watch a videotape of King delivering this speech, or have someone read the speech aloud. Consider the speech in light of your criteria and evaluate its effectiveness.

3. Since "I Have a Dream" is a speech and not an essay, Dr. King must make sure his audience understands his message immediately, as they won't have the opportunity to refer to the text. Analyze the techniques he uses to build a cumulative oral argument.

4. Discuss the current status of African Americans in the United States. Argue whether or not King's dream of an America where "all men are created equal" has become a reality.

For a different perspective on King, we recommend Septima Clark's *Ready from Within*. This book, which primarily describes the literacy drive in several African American communities during this period, presents a candid portrait of King.

MALCOLM X
From The Autobiography of Malcolm X

Students who are unfamiliar with Malcolm X might be interested in how he taught himself to read in prison by going through the dictionary and working his way through the prison library alphabetically and later became a leader in the black separatist movement. We chose this selection because it represents Malcolm X's position on nonviolence. Students should understand that position as well as his stand on Christianity in general. Then they can compare it to those of King and other advocates of nonviolent solutions to problems.

After reading, you can follow up with question 1, which asks students to articulate Malcolm X's position on nonviolence and the appropriate use of violence. This can serve as the basis for a debate between King and Malcolm X supporters. You might present Malcolm X as an example of someone who weathered the hardships of his upbringing and compare him to Rose in Chapter 9, who similarly achieved academically despite early problems. What motivated these men to overcome the obstacles that society had placed in their paths?

Question 3 raises the peripheral issue of whether Malcolm X and many other leaders of the civil rights movement focused exclusively on men. If you choose to pursue this topic, you might consider the role of women in the movement. Female leaders were not highly visible. Rosa Parks, though important, was not part of the power structure. Coretta King did not become a leader of the movement until after her husband's death. Was women's absence from the leadership a factor of the period (pre–women's movement), or did it result from the attitudes of male leaders? Were women active in other civil rights movements such as the organizations for migrant workers or the red power movement?

For additional information on women's roles in the civil rights movement, see Septima Clark's *Ready from Within*. Research question 2 at the end of the chapter also deals with this issue.

♦ Responding

1. Clarify Malcolm X's position on nonviolence and on the appropriate use of violence. Respond to his statement that "when the law fails to protect negroes from whites' attack, then those Negroes should use arms, if necessary, to defend themselves."

2. Working individually or in a group, list Malcolm X's criticisms of the Christian church. Do you think his charges are valid?

3. Discuss Malcolm X's solution to the problems of the "black man" around the world. Consider the strengths and weaknesses of that solution.

4. Argue in support of or against the position stated in the following passage: "It's the American political, economic, and social *atmosphere* that automatically nourishes a racist psychology in the white man. . . . American society makes it next to impossible for humans to meet in America and not be conscious of their color differences."

GWENDOLYN BROOKS
The Chicago Defender Sends a Man to Little Rock; Medgar Evers; Malcolm X

The Chicago Defender Sends a Man to Little Rock
This poem provides a good example of how one's own knowledge enhances one's reading. Students may need more information than the text offers to appreciate the poem. However, they might want to read the poem first and see what they can glean without understanding the context. Students who are familiar with this history undoubtedly will perceive the poem differently than those who are not.

You might explain that "New Criticism," which was popular until recently (and may have been the critical model for students' high school teachers) argued that a piece of writing could stand on its own and a reader needed no outside information about the period or the author to understand it. Then students can compare that approach with the approach taken in this text: that without understanding the context in which something is written, understanding of the writing is diminished or impossible. This poem presents a strong argument for that principle, and the following information seems crucial to understanding the piece.

Central High School in Little Rock, Arkansas, was chosen as the only school to be integrated in the Arkansas plan to comply with *Brown* v. *The Board of Education.* Nine black students were allowed to enroll in the school in the fall of 1957. However, white opposition led by governor Orvil Faubus tried to block integration by claiming that integrating the school would result in violence and surrounded the school with National Guard troops to prevent integration. When the nine students tried to attend school on the second day, they were confronted by a white mob that harassed them and blocked their entrance. The courts ordered Faubus to remove the National Guard, but the mob persisted. The school did not become integrated until President Eisenhower sent in federal troops. On September 23, 1957, four African American journalists from the *Chicago Defender,* a leading black newspaper, went to Central High School to report on the reception of the black students. The white bystanders mistook them for parents escorting their children to school and chased and attacked them.

The poem carries through King's and Farmer's themes of the "mob mentality" and the irony of the evil that exists in seemingly normal societies. Questions 2, 3, or 4 can help focus a post-reading discussion.

♦ Responding

1. Why does the poem begin with the date, "Fall, 1957"? Is it necessary to know about the events in Little Rock in order to understand the poem? What else does the poet expect her audience to know?

2. Describe the speaker. Who is he? For whom does he work? Is he white or black? How does he feel about what is happening?

3. Working individually or in a group, describe the people to whom the poet refers. Do they include the entire population of Little Rock?

4. Describe a time when you or someone you know became aware of an incident of injustice. What response did you or your friend have? Did you try to rectify what you felt was wrong? Were you successful or unsuccessful?

Medgar Evers
The introduction to the chapter recounts the tragedy of Evers's death. Students might want to review it before reading the poem.

♦ Responding

1. After reading the poem, research the events that made Medgar Evers a public figure and write a brief biography of him. Read the poem again after completing your research. In an essay, discuss the ways in which your additional knowledge changed your response to the poem.

2. In a brief essay, explain what you think Brooks means when she says Evers "leaned across tomorrow."

3. Write your own tribute to an important person in the public eye or in your personal life.

Malcolm X
If students have not read the excerpt from *The Autobiography of Malcolm X*, they might at least read the headnote to that piece prior to reading this poem. Information from that selection will be useful in answering question 1.

♦ Responding

1. Why does Brooks call Malcolm X "original"? Use information from your own knowledge or from other readings to support your answer.

2. Working individually or in a group, discuss the characteristics associated with maleness. How does Brooks use the term in this poem?

3. Discuss the poet's attitude toward her subject. Support your opinions with evidence from the poem.

JUAN WILLIAMS
From Eyes on the Prize

Our purpose in using this reading is to bring students up to date and help them assess the effects of the civil rights movement on the various branches of government and on the public. As a pre-reading activity, you might ask a question about change: What lasting effects did the civil rights movement have, and what changes are still being resisted? Students may want to look at the timeline constructed during the Beginning exercise to evaluate which events produced lasting effects and which were superficial. Williams feels that the Voting Rights Act produced many benefits. Students can review the actions the southern states took to keep African Americans from voting and having a say in legislation, the sacrifices that were made to gain those rights, and the difficulties civil rights leaders encountered in attempting to change attitudes.

Question 1 can introduce a discussion of the success of the Voting Rights Act. Some students may feel that things have changed little since the 1960s despite new legislation, that racism still exists in this country. That argument could be used as the focus of a follow-up discussion.

Another approach would be to have students look at related issues such as affirmative action, equal opportunity, and other antidiscriminatory legislation and discuss whether such legislation has succeeded in changing attitudes. To do this, students must be familiar with the laws, so you may have to provide them with copies or summaries. Alternatively they could investigate affirmative action programs on their own campus. They might interview administrators to learn the rationale behind the programs and how the programs are implemented. Their familiarity with the problems African Americans have faced in getting education, jobs, and housing should help them understand some of the thinking behind affirmative action programs. Students might also want to read Richard Rodriguez, an opponent of affirmative action. Questions 2 and 3 would be helpful in such a discussion.

Question 2 might work well as a small- or large-group follow-up discussion topic. Question 3 could be used to sum up the chapter and might begin or follow a discussion of racism in America today.

♦ Responding

1. Restate Williams's reasons for thinking that the Voting Rights Act was highly influential and significant.

2. Argue for or against the idea that though morality cannot be controlled by legislation, the passage of laws can gradually change attitudes.

3. Working individually or in a group, discuss the shift in focus that took place in the civil rights movement after 1965. List the civil rights issues that seem most important today. Share your list with the class.

CONNECTING (printed in AMERICAN MOSAIC, p. 471)

Critical Thinking and Writing

The connecting questions link ideas and themes within this chapter and the entire text. For example, questions 1, 2, 11, and 12 ask students to trace a theme throughout the text while 3, 5, and 8 suggest comparisons within the chapter. Question 9 asks for a specific comparison with material from the introduction to

Chapter 9 and might call for outside reading. In addition, some questions suggest ties between the readings in this chapter and the presentation of the same issues in other media. Questions 4 and 7 ask students to discuss the readings in relation to specific films.

The research questions focus specifically on women, civil rights leaders, and the history of civil disobedience. These might be modified into topics for shorter papers.

For hints about using the questions see the connecting questions section of Chapter 1 in this manual.

CHAPTER 7

CHICANOS: NEGOTIATING ECONOMIC AND CULTURAL BOUNDARIES

This chapter chronicles some of the experiences of Chicanos in the United States. Students need to read the introduction to the chapter to understand the long history of Mexicans in the Southwest. *Chicanos* are defined as people of Mexican descent born and raised in the United States. While some of the characters in the stories are Mexican migrant workers or Mexican nationals, their children are Chicano. (Like other group names, *Chicano* currently is the center of controversy. Some people view it as derogatory and prefer *Latino, Hispanic*, or *Mexican American*. However, *Chicano* is the appropriate term for the time period of these readings.) We hope that these readings, like all those in the text, present a sufficiently wide range of characters, attitudes, and behaviors that students will rethink any stereotypical ideas about groups. Here we want students to appreciate the important role Mexican culture plays in the lives of Chicanos (and throughout the United States) without reinforcing persistent stereotypes.

Beginning: Pre-reading/Writing

Working individually or in a group, list examples of Mexican culture that you encounter in your daily life. Consider the following: food, clothing, language, architecture, holidays, art, and music. Share examples with the class and discuss the ways in which Mexican culture enriches American culture.

The Beginning exercise aims to make students aware of the enriching influence of Mexican culture on their lives. Throughout the United States, Mexican food abounds and Mexican music (e.g., "La Bamba") has reached the pop charts. A possible follow-up question is to ask students to consider how food, art, music, and so on have changed upon crossing the border. Students who have visited Mexico or are of Mexican descent can be the experts. You might point out how much richer Mexican culture is than that depicted in stereotypical representations. Mexican food, for example, goes far beyond tacos and enchiladas, and Mexican Indian dress and crafts vary in different regions of the country.

From The Treaty of Guadalupe Hidalgo

This excerpt is interesting because of the promises it makes and its illustrations of the changes forced on the Mexican people living in the ceded areas. The article in the treaty guaranteeing Mexican citizens their rights to property, religion, and liberty was never passed by Congress. You might have students compare this treaty to the broken promises in the treaties between the United States and the American Indians (see Lincoln in Chapter 8).

Question 1 aims to make students aware of the history of the Southwest. Some students may not know that during the period of the westward movement, Mexican settlers predated Europeans and were the majority in much of the Southwest, Texas, and California. Have them review the introduction to the chapter and use outside sources if necessary.

Question 2 might begin the post-reading discussion. You could ask students how they would feel if they suddenly found themselves living in a place that a neighboring country had taken over. What would their concerns be?

♦ Responding

1. Determine which parts of the United States were originally settled by Mexico. How did they become American territory?

2. Discuss the effects of the Treaty of Guadalupe Hidalgo on Mexicans living in the disputed area. What rights were they guaranteed? What did they have to give up?

JOSÉ ANTONIO VILLAREAL
From Pocho

This reading points up a conflict between the values of immigrant parents and their children raised in America. At the same time, it counters the pervasive belief that Chicanos are not interested in education. Like Richard, students may have conflicts with their families regarding education. For some, the conflict may have evolved because they are the first generation to attend college; for others, the conflict may have resulted from their parents pushing them in directions they are unwilling to go. A possible pre-reading question is to have students think about a time when their goals conflicted with their parents' and discuss the difficulties that ensued. If you choose this approach, you may want to follow up with question 3 or 4. Question 3 is quite text specific. If your class chooses this exercise, they should know that *Pocho* is an outdated, derogatory name that Chicanos formerly used for members of their community who tried to assimilate into the mainstream at the expense of their identities. After discussing question 3, students can discuss whether this term would fit Richard. Question 4 asks students to make a more personal statement; this may work well as the topic for a journal entry.

Alternatively, your class may read this selection for what it says about the purpose of education, another recurring theme in this text. A pre-reading activity might consist of asking students why they are in college or what they considered when choosing a major. As a post-reading activity, students may wish to discuss question 1. The discussion can be expanded to bring in the informal education the *tabaqueros* received in the Vega reading in Chapter 4. Question 2 offers an opportunity for a more creative follow-up.

♦ Responding

1. This reading presents two views of education. Richard argues that "If I were to go to school only to learn to work at something, then I would not do it." His mother responds, "If you could go to the university, it would be to learn how you could make more money than you would make in the fields or the cannery." Discuss the merits of each point of view.

2. What do you think Richard will be doing in ten years? Do you think he will quit school, or will he finish his education? Write a story about Richard that takes place ten years after this episode ends.

3. Several value systems come into conflict in this story. Working individually or in a group, list the values of Richard, his mother, his father, and their community. Compare your list with those of other classmates and discuss how values shape behavior and what possible conflicts between family members can arise.

4. Richard's parents want him to have a better life than they have. Would your parents like your life to be different from theirs? In what ways? How do your wishes and plans for your future differ from theirs? How do you and your parents cope with these differences?

CÉSAR CHÁVEZ
The Organizer's Tale

This reading, like the two selections that follow, addresses the experiences of migrant workers. This is an important aspect of Chicano history because many Mexicans came to the United States as migrant workers. An effective way to introduce their situation would be to show the Edward R. Murrow video *Harvest of Shame.* You might begin by asking students what they know about the food they eat: Do they understand that some crops must be harvested by hand and how difficult that work is? Students who have read Steinbeck's *The Grapes of Wrath* or seen the film version might introduce this work into the discussion.

Before reading "The Organizer's Tale," students might find it helpful to review the events of the McCarthy era. Some students may have little knowledge of this period, and this additional information can make them more aware of the risks Chávez and his fellow workers took when they decided to fight for their rights. As a post-reading activity, you can use question 2.

An alternative is to examine the development of Chávez's organization. Following a general discussion about the plight of the migrant workers, you might ask students to list the things they would consider changing first if they were going to live and work under the conditions of the migrant workers. After reading the selection, students can examine how Chávez approached this problem by looking at questions 1, 3, and 4.

Question 1 could also be used to focus follow-up activities. Working individually or in a group, students could isolate the specific techniques Chávez learned.

Question 4 can be answered adequately from material in the essay, but some outside reading would be helpful. It is important that students understand the significance of Chávez and the United Farm Workers. Current issues facing the union include concerns over pesticides and other cancer-causing additives.

◆ Responding

1. Identify what Chávez learned that helped him become a labor organizer.

2. Research the McCarthy era. What does Chávez mean when he says he was "subjected to a lot of redbaiting"?

3. Chávez says, "Whatever you do, and no matter what reasons you may give to others, you do it because you want to see it done, or maybe because you want power." Agree or disagree with this statement. Use examples from the essay to support your argument.

4. Review the philosophy, focus, and methods of the organization Chávez founded. Discuss the advantages and disadvantages of his method of going directly to the people.

TOMÁS RIVERA
La Nocha Buena/Christmas Eve

This selection, like the story by Ulibarrí later in the chapter, has been reprinted in both Spanish and English because it was originally written in Spanish and the English version is a translation. For readers of both languages, the side-by-side text adds enrichment. The story brings up a recurring theme in this text, the difficulties individuals face when they are in an alien culture or feel unable to deal with circumstances. For a post-reading activity, students might compare doña María's reactions to those of Santos in "Ropes of Passage" (Chapter 4) or Beret in "Facing the Great Desolation" (Chapter 1). Both doña María and Beret become overwhelmed by the challenge of adjusting to a new world, and they can be compared to the many women who cope well. The selections by Ulibarrí and Cisneros in this chapter are other possible resources.

To answer question 1, students can write a ten-minute in-class response discussing Rivera's and their own attitudes toward doña María. Where do their sympathies lie, and why? Then they can share their responses with the class. Question 2 may work well as a follow-up to this discussion.

Another aspect of this story concerns how society looks at people who have difficulty fitting in. Do they tend to make it easier for outsiders to become part of the mainstream, or do they inhibit them? Question 4 could be used to initiate this topic. A class discussion of the onlookers' various points of view will help students understand the ways in which economic, cultural, and political issues can affect one's viewpoint.

◆ Responding

1. Discuss Rivera's attitude toward doña María. Is he sympathetic or unsympathetic? How does he try to get the reader to share his viewpoint?

2. Have you ever been afraid to do something or tried to do something that was very threatening and failed in the attempt? How did you feel about yourself? Did you try again? How does doña María feel about her attempt to go to the store? Do you think she will try again?

3. What is the attitude of the person who stops doña María outside the store? What do this person's comments reveal about attitudes toward the migrant community?

4. Pretend that you are one of the following people in the crowd around doña María: a local banker, the store owner, the guard, a friend, a migrant worker, one of doña María's children, a local reporter, a reporter from a large metropolitan area, a civil rights worker. Write a letter to a friend or to the editor of the local paper about the incident.

ANA CASTILLO
Napa, California; Milagros

Napa, California
Before students read the poem, you should explain that the dashes serve as
question marks, suggesting several speakers. As the translation shows, a child
asks the mother, "Well, Mom, what should we do now?" The mother replies, "Let's
follow him." The class may wish to read this dialogue aloud, assigning parts. The
implication is that at last the workers have a leader who has gained their trust.

"Napa, California" was written in tribute to Cézar Chávez. You might have
students read the poem when they read the Chávez piece and follow up with a
discussion of question 1. Students might want to discuss this tribute and compare
it to Brooks's poetic tribute in Chapter 6 and Mirikitani's in Chapter 5. Mirikitani
and Castillo wrote their works long after the events. Would this make a difference
in their treatment or their perspectives?

Questions 3 and 4 ask students to consider the poem in relation to its audience
and to analyze the effects the poet is trying to achieve. The questions also could be
used as post-reading activities.

♦ **Responding**

1. Understanding a poem often means understanding the poem's references to
    events and people. Research the title and dedication of this poem. Why did the
    poet choose "Napa," "Sr. Chávez," and "sept. '75"? Reflect on the role of titles
    and the information they provide the reader. What might some alternate titles
    for this poem be? What response might these titles produce in a reader?

2. What is the "we" in the poem? What information does the poem give you about
    these people?

3. Copy one stanza of the poem into conventional prose sentences. How is the
    effect different? Discuss the reasons why the poet may have written the
    stanzas in the form she did.

4. Reread the translation of the Spanish text. Why do you think the author
    includes several lines in Spanish? How did you react when you first read these
    lines?

Milagros
"Milagros" presents another woman who has dreams for the future but probably
will never realize them. She stands between the characters who are beaten down
by circumstances (see the comments to "Christmas Eve") and those who fight those
circumstances. After reading this poem, students might use question 1 to
speculate about her future. They can use question 3 to discuss how her future may

be shaped by her husband.

♦ Responding

1. Do you think Milagros's dreams of going back home and getting an education will come true? What do you think the poet believes?

2. Compare the treatment of the repeated line "where her baby sleeps." What do you think the poet may be trying to suggest by changing the format? Do you respond to the line differently at each repetition? How?

3. Milagros's husband doesn't appear in the poem, but we hear about him. What clues does the poem give us about his attitudes toward the United States, the role of women, and the family?

4. Who is Milagros talking to? Working in a group, describe the speaker and write a scenario explaining who this person is and what his or her relationship is to Milagros.

PAT MORA
Illegal Alien; Legal Alien

Despite the pairing of the titles, these two poems need not be considered together.

Illegal Alien

"Illegal Alien" brings up the theme of wife beating that recurs in the Cisneros story that follows. It also gives a one-sided view of the relationship between employer and employee, native and nonnative. Students might want to try question 2 or 3 as a post-reading activity. Either question could lead to a further discussion of the relationships suggested in the poem and by the questions.

♦ Responding

1. What relationship do the two women in the poem have? What does the relationship mean to the speaker? What images in the poem help the reader to understand the poet's attitude toward the narrator and Socorro?

2. Imagine that Socorro has written to one of the following people for help in dealing with her physically abusive husband: her mother, a social worker,

"Dear Abby," a religious leader, an administrator of a shelter for battered women. Write a reply from the point of view of that person.

3. We know what the speaker has to say but not what Socorro is thinking. Working with a partner, each taking one role, write a dialogue between Socorro and the speaker. Share your dialogue with your classmates.

4. What does being "women, both married, both warmed by Mexican blood" create between the two people in the poem? Does it make them responsible to each other for comfort and guidance?

Legal Alien

Before students read "Legal Alien," they might define the term *bicultural*. After reading the poem, they can compare the speaker's situation with that in any of the other readings, such as Lowe (Chapter 2) and Okada (Chapter 5). This could be followed by a discussion of question 2.

♦ Responding

1. Is "legal alien" a contradiction in terms? What does the speaker mean when she calls herself a legal alien?

2. The speaker believes that being bicultural means that you aren't really accepted by either culture. Do you agree or disagree? Support your position by referring to the poem, other readings in the text, or your experience.

3. Tell about a time when you or someone you know felt torn between two traditions, two sets of beliefs, or two cultures.

4. Working individually or in a group, list the advantages and disadvantages of being bicultural in the United States today. Compare notes with the class. Write an essay presenting your conclusions.

SABINE ULIBARRÍ
Mi Abuela Fumaba Puros/My Grandma Smoked Cigars

Ulibarrí's story portrays a strong woman who knows how to handle life's problems. Before students read it, you might review with them some of the other women characters they have encountered in the text, particularly in this chapter. A more detailed discussion might follow the reading.

If you want to analyze the grandmother before comparing her to other female characters, you might follow the reading with the activity proposed in question 1.

After a comparison of the lists, you could ask each group to choose one of the other women characters they discussed in the pre-reading activity and do the same thing. A follow-up in-class writing assignment would be to ask students to compare the characters they selected to the grandmother: How culture based are similarities and differences? What are the effects of social status, language, country of birth, and era on an individual's personality?

If students prefer to take a less encompassing approach to the reading, they might concentrate on one or two aspects of the grandmother's personality, such as her reaction to grief; question 3 can be helpful here. Students can also compare her responses with those of the grandmother in the selection from *Love Medicine* in Chapter 8.

♦ Responding

1. Ulibarrí's verbal portrait of his grandmother draws on significant details that reveal her personality and character. Working individually or in a group, review the information he gives and compile a list of his grandmother's character traits. Compare your list with those of other groups.

2. Ulibarrí's grandmother had a special significance in his life. Write a character sketch of someone you admire who has influenced you. Through your selection of details, try to illustrate and dramatize why you regard this person as a good role model.

3. Write an essay supporting Ulibarrí's statement that his grandmother "had dominated the harsh reality in which she lived."

4. Write an essay arguing that the grandmother is both very dominating and very sentimental. Support your argument with evidence from the reading.

ARTURO ISLAS
From Migrant Souls

This selection from Islas's novel brings up issues that reflect current concerns in American society: defining the physical and psychological border between the United States and Mexico; racial prejudice within a group toward members who possess characteristics such as skin color, language, or behavior that fit the mainstream's stereotype of that group; racial prejudice by the majority who want to restrict members of the group by limiting their entry into the country or their opportunities for jobs and housing. To more fully understand the situation of Mexican Americans living on the border and what they must face when they try to cross into what was once their homeland or is the home of relatives, students can review the history of the border discussed in the introduction to the chapter. It is important for them to understand that for many Mexicans and Mexican Americans, the border is an arbitrary line.

This reading, like others in the text, openly acknowledges the existence of prejudice within a racial group. Because all racial groups have such prejudices, you might have a pre-reading discussion about these feelings and perhaps speculate on how they have evolved. After reading this selection, students might want to compare the mother's attitudes with those depicted in the excerpt from *The Blacker the Berry* in Chapter 3.

Islas also tackles the issue of names and their ability to distort thinking and inflict pain. This echoes many of the concerns of the civil rights period. Students might review the Beginning exercise from Chapter 6 before reading. These are current concerns for many groups. Takaki (Chapter 5) discusses how the issue relates to the Japanese American.

If students want to discuss prejudice from without and its effects, they can refer to question 5, which asks them to consider the effects of the deportation stories on the children who live on the border. Some also may have been raised with stories like these or with stories that evoked other fears such as fear of different ethnic groups. Students may feel comfortable discussing those fears. If they do not, this might be a good entree into a discussion of the mistrust and fear that often poison relations among people.

Any of these issues may be used to begin the pre-reading or post-reading discussion. However, the piece also has a humorous side, which students may want to discuss; question 4 offers a suitable post-reading activity.

♦ Responding

1. Compare the mother's attitudes toward American Indians and Mexican Indians. Why might someone find her statements ironic? Do you think her views are widespread in American society?

2. Explain Sancho's reaction to the term *alien*. How does he define the term, and why is it so offensive to him? Write an essay explaining why his reaction is or is not excessive. Or write an essay speculating about Sancho's reaction to Mora's poems "Legal Alien" and "Illegal Alien."

3. Working individually or in a group, list examples of the bicultural aspects of the Angel family's lifestyle. Discuss the advantages and disadvantages of being bicultural.

4. Taking the turkey over the border can be viewed as humorous, serious, or even frightening, depending on your point of view. Imagine you are one of the characters in the story and report the incident to a friend.

5. "The Angel children were brought up on as many deportation stories as fairy tales and family legends." Discuss the possible psychological effects of such stories on young children.

SANDRA CISNEROS
Woman Hollering Creek

Here is another reading that deals with women in difficult situations. At first we felt the writer had led us to believe that the story would have a negative ending, and we were pleased with the turn of events. The story presents an all too familiar situation — a woman far from family and friends — that usually has a very unhappy outcome. But this woman, unlike Socorro in "Illegal Alien," acts. She can be compared to other women in the text who act, such as Delia in "Sweat" (Chapter 3) and Amy in "A Thanksgiving Celebration" (Chapter 4).

A pre-reading discussion might ask students to define women's roles in various cultures. The Allen selection in Chapter 8 is a good resource. What are the responsibilities of a wife and mother? Which responsibility is primary? What are the responsibilities of a husband? What should a woman do if she is abused or mistreated by her husband?

The post-reading activities might begin with students writing in class for ten minutes about their responses to Cleófilas's actions. Was she right to leave? What might have happened had she stayed? This might lead to a discussion of different images and role models for women such as Felice. Any of the four questions would work well as a follow-up to the writing.

Students might enjoy writing a different ending for the story (Question 3). They can write the endings individually or in a group, as a story or as a scene between any of the characters. Then they can read their endings in class and compare them to the original ending.

♦ **Responding**

1. Compare Cleófilas's situation and Graciela's response to it with Socorro's situation and the speaker's response in Mora's poem "Illegal Alien."

2. Why does Cleófilas think that "Felice was like no woman she'd ever met"? Is that observation a compliment or a criticism? Explain Cleófilas's attitude toward Felice.

3. Analyze the appeal of the *telenovelas* for Cleófilas. If her story appeared on a soap opera, how might the ending differ? Write an alternate ending for the story, and discuss it with the class. In an essay, explain which ending you like best and why.

4. Cleófilas acts to remove herself and her child from a dangerous situation.
    Write about a time when you or someone you know or have read about took a
    risk to make a bad situation better.

HÉCTOR CALDERÓN
Reinventing the Border

This essay about Calderón's experiences growing up on the border between
California and Mexico could be introduced by referring to the children in the
selection from Islas. Islas creates a fictional world from his own knowledge and
experience; Calderón talks about his own life in a similar world. For both the
fictional and nonfictional characters, the border looms as a significant influence on
their attitudes and their lives. You might have students think carefully about
what it means to live on a border and to be part of the cultures on both sides (see
question 1). Students could extend the image of the border to other, nonphysical
aspects of life: borders between people, professions, states of mind, and so forth.
Question 3, which asks students to define *border*, might serve as a focus for a
small- or large-group follow-up discussion.

♦ Responding

1. Explain what Calderón means when he says "we were reminded of both what
    we were and what we were not."

2. Discuss the way in which Lummis romanticized the Southwest. Compare his
    version of history with the presentations in the other readings in this chapter.

3. Define *border*. Compare your definition with Calderón's.

4. Calderón reports that many of his daily and seasonal activities as a child were
    "dictated by Mexican oral and written tradition, handed down to our family by
    our grandmother." Write an essay about the influence of cultural or family
    traditions on your childhood.

CONNECTING (printed in AMERICAN MOSAIC, p. 563)

Critical Thinking and Writing

Several of the questions in this set can work in pairs (1 and 2, 5 and 6, and 7 and
8). The first questions in each pair, numbers 1, 5, and 7, ask students to consider

specific topics using information from this chapter. The second questions, numbers 2, 6, and 8, ask students to discuss the topic within the text as a whole. Questions 9 and 10, however, bring up general issues that recur throughout the text.

The research questions give students an opportunity to find out more about the recent history and concerns of Chicanos.

Brief suggestions for using the connecting questions appear in Chapter 1 of this manual.

CHAPTER 8

NATIVE AMERICANS: PRIDE AND CULTURAL HERITAGE

This chapter presents selections by Native American writers during the period that has been called the Native American Renaissance, an outgrowth of the civil rights movement of the 1960s. The rebirth of interest in Native American culture reflects Americans' awareness of the importance of cultural heritage and the movement toward cultural pluralism and away from a melting-pot orientation.

The introduction to the chapter reviews the history of Native American tribes' contact with white people and the resulting difficulties they faced in maintaining land, heritage, and even family.

Each author represented in the chapter is from a different tribe. It is important for students to realize that Native Americans come from diverse tribes and cultures. Students should read the introduction but might discuss the Beginning exercise beforehand.

Beginning: Pre-reading/Writing

Critics charge that Native Americans have often been stereotyped in films and in television series as vicious savages or as romanticized innocents. Working individually or in a group, list the general characteristics attributed to Native Americans in early Westerns, specific television series, and commercials. Has the portrayal changed over time? If so, in what ways? As you read the chapter, compare these depictions with those by Native American authors.

	Characteristics		
Men	Film	Television	Commercials
Physical appearance			
Personality			
Character traits			
Behavior			
Clothing			
Work			
Hobbies			

	Characteristics		
Women	*Film*	*Television*	*Commercials*
Physical appearance			
Personality			
Character traits			
Behavior			
Clothing			
Work			
Hobbies			

Because students probably have seen images of Native Americans in the media, they may think they know a great deal about them. A recent example portrays an Indian with tears in his eyes as he views the polluted landscape. But is this a realistic or a romanticized portrayal? The Beginning exercise aims to alert students to the diversity among Native Americans and to dispel common stereotypes. Encourage them to explore their preconceptions and check them against the portrayals in the readings.

From The Indian Removal Act

The document presented here is a section of the Removal Act of 1830. We felt that it is an important reading because it clearly exemplifies how the American government treated the Native Americans. It also focuses on the potential effects of forced removal on a people's sense of identity. Students might begin by discussing what it means to be forced to leave one's ancestral land. Some students may have ancestors who endured forced emigration (e.g., blacks forced to leave Africa or others forced to emigrate by political or religious persecution). The Lincoln reading that ends the chapter chronicles many of the broken promises between the United States government and the tribes. If your students wish to focus on the government's treatment of Native Americans, they can speculate about the government's motives for uprooting an entire nation before they read the selection.

Implicit in the Removal Act was the belief that Native Americans soon would become extinct. The Responding questions aim to make students aware of this by having them look closely at the language and construction of the document. Section 3 provides that lands will revert to the United States "if the Indians become extinct, or abandon the same." If students already discussed the effects of being forced from ancestral lands, you can discuss how such a separation could contribute to the extinction of a people.

♦ Responding

1. Working individually or in a group, paraphrase and list the provisions of the Act. Share your list with the class and discuss what the provisions meant to the people affected.

2. Discuss the government's assumptions about the future of Native Americans implicit in the document. Support your opinions with evidence from the Act.

3. Research the myth of the "vanishing American." Using evidence from the Act, argue that the legislators who wrote this bill did or did not give credence to this myth.

N. SCOTT MOMADAY
January 26

We chose this reading because it portrays Native Americans in an urban rather than rural setting. Its blending of Christianity and paganism and its focus on attitudes toward language present many possibilities for discussion and comparison. The importance of storytelling, suggested in earlier chapters (e.g., Chapter 4) is prominent here as well.

Depending on the focus the class has selected, a number of pre- and post-reading activities are available. One pre-reading activity could have students write or discuss the importance of storytelling in their own families or cultures. In a post-reading discussion, they could compare the role of storytelling in their own lives with that in the lives of the Priest of the Sun and his grandmother. Following this, students may want to try question 4.

The interweaving of Christianity and paganism, a dominant aspect of Native American culture, also might interest students. Before reading the selection, students can discuss how many Christian traditions, such as Christmas trees, Halloween, Easter eggs, and so forth, had their origins in paganism; how did they cross over into Christianity? As a post-reading activity, students can list Christian and pagan influences in the reading. Discussion might focus on the problems, if any, of reconciling the two influences. This also can serve as a pre-writing exercise for question 2. For another example of the blending of Christianity and a Native American religion, see the excerpt from *Love Medicine* in this chapter.

Another important aspect of the Native American Renaissance is the recent Pan-Indian movement, which has helped overcome tribal differences and has given Native Americans a greater power base. Question 1 helps to focus attention on this movement and asks students to consider the attitudes of the native people. Students might review the devastating effects of the Removal Act. How can Pan-Indian unity help contribute to the survival of a native people? What, if anything, is lost in solidarity?

♦ **Responding**

1. The signboard on the building where the Priest of the Sun gives his sermon reads "Holiness Pan-Indian Rescue Mission." Using information from the introduction to the chapter, define Pan-Indian and explain why that term would have been unusual before 1960. What changes in attitudes does it reflect?

2. Write an essay discussing the cultural conflicts that Native Americans face in trying to adopt Christianity while retaining their own religion.

3. Explain the ways in which the Priest of the Sun believes the white man's use of "the Word" differs from the Kiowas'. Use examples from the reading and your own knowledge to illustrate the differences. Write an essay or a journal entry agreeing or disagreeing with the Priest's conclusions.

4. Are stories an important way of transmitting knowledge in your family, or among friends? Tell a story that teaches a cultural lesson.

LESLIE MARMON SILKO
Lullaby

This touching story illustrates some of the difficulties Native Americans experienced as a result of the government policies described in the introduction. It also deals with a number of themes explored throughout the text: the problems that can develop when people of a minority culture don't speak the same language or live by the same customs as those in the majority culture; the frustrations in dealing with a bureaucracy; the loss of children to a "foreign" culture; the inability of minority members to be fully accepted by the mainstream even if they follow the "rules."

As a pre-reading activity, students might share experiences in which a misunderstanding of language and customs created difficulties. After reading, questions 1 and 4 give students a creative means for exploring this problem through writing. This could lead to a discussion of the rights of the state versus the rights of the family. Students could bring in current news stories about Native American tribes who have struggled to reclaim children adopted away from the tribe. Question 4 could serve as a ten-minute in-class writing assignment. Students can also write about their emotional responses to the story.

One approach to this reading involves examining the problems created by the inability to communicate, both linguistically and conceptually. Another possibility is to discuss the problems people sometimes encounter when dealing with a bureaucracy like the government or a university. A follow-up discussion could touch on the viewpoint of the government and the arguments on Ayah's side. A possible discussion or debate topic is the right of institutions to interfere in family life for the "good" of minor children. The parents' plight could be compared to that of the family in Far's "In the Land of the Free" (Chapter 2). The children in both stories in effect have been stolen from their parents and their culture.

Another approach is to look at this story from the viewpoint of those who try to assimilate into the mainstream. Chato worked well in the white person's world, but in the end he still is thrown aside. Question 2 will help in exploring this issue. Students may be interested in comparing Chato with Pardee Lowe in Chapter 2: In what ways is their disappointment similar? How does it differ?

♦ Responding

1. Working with a partner, write a dialogue between Ayah and the doctor who comes to take away her children. If he spoke her language, what argument would he use to convince her to consent to having the children taken away for treatment? How would she respond?

2. Chato ends his life destitute, spending his government checks on alcohol. Discuss the causes of his difficulties. In your opinion, who is responsible for his problems?

3. Explain Ayah's attitude toward life and death, illustrating your explanation with examples from the text.

4. The action takes place "back in the days before they hired Navajo women to go with them as interpreters." Ayah loses her children because she doesn't speak English and can't read the paper she is given to sign. In a journal entry, describe your reactions to these tragic events, or tell about a time when you or someone you know was in a situation in which lack of understanding of language or customs created great difficulties.

JAMES WELCH
Plea to Those Who Matter; Riding the Earthboy 40

These two poems explore the issues of tradition and identity.

Plea to Those Who Matter
Students should be made aware of the social pressures on Native Americans to conform to Euro-American standards of beauty and behavior. This is an issue that has faced and still faces members of ethnic minorities. In the excerpt from *"The Blacker the Berry"* (Chapter 3), the heroine values lighter skin and what she believes is appropriate behavior. All ethnic groups have been pressured at some

time to straighten hair and noses, lighten skin, and tone down behavior to fit an Anglo-Saxon image. Movements such as the "Black Is Beautiful movement" of the 1960s tried to counter that pressure. A pre-reading discussion could focus on these issues or ask students if they have ever felt obligated to strive for a certain image. Students have told us that criteria such as these still influence their self-image. Question 3 could be used as a follow-up activity.

◆ Responding

1. Identify and describe the speaker in the poem. According to the poem, who are "the ones who matter"? How is the speaker willing to change to please them?

2. Explain the attitude of the poet toward the speaker. Does he approve or disapprove of the speaker's behavior? Support your opinion by citing examples from the poem.

3. Working individually or with a partner, write a dialogue between the speaker and an Indian rights activist.

Riding the Earthboy 40
This poem uses mythology and tradition in a contemporary poem. Earthboy is a family name, and 40 is the acreage of the family's land holdings. Earthboy also calls to mind the mythical Earth-diver, a creature in North American Indian myths (and other folklore) of the origin of the world. In the myth, the hero has a succession of animals dive into the primeval waters and attempt to bring up bits of mud or sand. Most of the animals fail, but finally one brings up a tiny bit of sand or dirt. Magically this expands into the world. Another myth describes the creation of humankind from a similar substance.

You may wish to explain the references to Earthboy and 40 before students read the poem, or you could have them answer question 1 first. Question 1 asks them what additional information they need to enhance their understanding. Could they have guessed that Earthboy was a family name? Were they unable to guess because of their cultural bias toward certain types of names?

Knowledge of Native American mythology also might enrich the reading, but you may prefer to share this information after students have read the poem once. After this first reading, they might enjoy exploring the implications of the mythology. Question 2 can be interpreted in light of the creation myth, but that is only one possibility. There is no one correct reading; we believe students should respond to the poem and then consider various possibilities. The focus of the question is on what students think the speaker means.

♦ **Responding**

1. Who is the speaker in this poem and what attitude does he have toward the
    Earthboy? What additional information might enrich your reading of the
    poem?

2. What do you think the speaker means when he says "Earthboy calls me from
    my dream: Dirt is where the dreams must end"?

LOUISE ERDRICH
From Love Medicine

Because of the structure of the novel, this chapter can stand alone and be enjoyed
as a short story. One pre-reading activity is to ask students to recall a time when
they tried to do something to help someone and everything went wrong. You might
ask them how they felt when their good intentions went awry. This is what
happens to Lipsha Morrissey, but from the experience he reaches a new
understanding of life, death, and love. A post-reading discussion might begin by
focusing on what he learned; this topic also could be a ten-minute in-class writing
assignment. Question 4 extends this discussion. Students can use the in-class
discussion as pre-writing for a formal paper.

Another aspect of this story is Lipsha's belief in "the touch" and how he
reconciles it with Christianity. Questions 2 and 3 can be helpful in exploring this
theme. Lipsha's integration of Christianity and paganism could be compared to the
integration in the church in the Momaday reading.

♦ **Responding**

1. Lipsha Morrissey describes human behavior by comparing it to things he sees
    in the world around him. Find some of his descriptions and discuss what they
    tell you about his daily life. Replace some of his descriptions with ones of your
    own that reflect your understanding of human behavior.

2. The Catholic Church and the Chippewas' traditional beliefs make up a great
    deal of Lipsha's world view. Give some examples from the story that show how
    each influences his thinking and behavior and the ways in which he combines
    the two.

3. Explain why Lipsha views the U.S. government as a "Higher Power" or God.

4. Grandpa Kashpaw's death gives Lipsha a new understanding of life, death, and love. Using examples from the reading, discuss the changes that take place in his understanding of life's milestones.

PAULA GUNN ALLEN
Where I Come from Is Like This

Allen's piece directly addresses the issues of identity and femininity and the differing approaches of Native Americans and western civilizations. Because of the directness, this reading gives students ample opportunity to take a stand and either support or argue against Allen. You might begin with a pre-reading discussion about the topic of question 2: the definition of men's and women's roles in one's culture. Students should have enough material from their own experiences and from the readings to compare these roles now and in the past. A variation of the question is to ask students to examine the roles of men and women as portrayed in other readings in this or earlier chapters and compare those roles to today. A follow-up discussion answering question 1 can plug in Allen's assertions. Students may disagree with her claim that women are defined by western civilization. Does Allen romanticize women's role in Native American culture?

Allen also brings up the ongoing theme of stories and the oral tradition. This view can be compared to the Priest's in the Momaday reading or to other cultures in which storytelling is a way to preserve the culture. After reading the selection, you can look at question 3. Students may want to share their own stories by reading them aloud or duplicating them for circulation in the class. If duplicating funds are unavailable, a few copies can be made and circulated. Other oral traditions, from African genealogies to Homer to the Bible, can be discussed. The influence of the oral tradition is a theme that can be developed to tie in with the experiences of many groups. A further extension of this theme would be a discussion about what happens to these stories when they are written down: What changes and what remains the same?

Another ongoing theme that Allen explores is the plight of people who are constantly confronted with a negative self-image — an experience of many immigrant and minority groups. Question 4 would be a good follow-up with this approach. A discussion of Native Americans' sense of identity and self-esteem could easily extend to a discussion of these issues in relation to Japanese Americans, African Americans, Jewish Americans, and so forth.

♦ Responding

1. Allen asserts that "In the west, few images of women form part of the cultural mythos." Working individually or in a group, compare the way an American Indian woman is defined by her tribe with the way a woman is defined by

Western civilization. Summarize the most important differences and share these with the class. Write an essay or a journal entry agreeing or disagreeing with Allen's depiction of Western women's roles in their culture.

2. How are women's and men's roles defined in your culture? Compare current roles for men and women with those in your mother's and your grandmother's time.

3. Allen talks about the power of the oral tradition — the family stories passed down to her from her mother. Using examples from the reading, discuss the role of tradition in preserving a culture. Consider the stories or traditions that have been passed down in your family. Do your stories tell you, as Allen's told her, "who I was, who I was supposed to be, whom I came from, and who would follow me"? Write or tell one of your own important family stories.

4. According to Allen, "no Indian can grow to any age without being informed that her people were 'savages' who interfered with the march of progress pursued by respectable, loving, civilized white people." Consider the source or impetus behind such messages. What effects might such a portrayal have on a Native American's sense of identity and self-esteem?

KENNETH LINCOLN
Old Like Hills, Like Stars

Lincoln's piece reviews Native Americans' tragic experiences with the United States government. It also tries to dispel common stereotypes. Students should be aware that the portrayal of Native Americans changed after the 1960s. Prior to the greater awareness of civil rights issues, Native Americans usually were portrayed as savages harming innocent white settlers. Students might want to outline that history as they read and use it to begin the post-reading discussion. If they have seen enough old Westerns on television, they might compare that version of history with Lincoln's. Such a discussion could lead into a reintroduction of the Beginning exercise. Now that students have read all the other selections in this chapter, they can compare their preconceptions with those portraits. Question 11 in the Connecting section focuses on "misdirected romanticism." You should stress that these too are merely individual writers' impressions and should not be used to stereotype the group. For question 1 in the Responding section, you may have to repeat the point that a culture may have certain characteristics and people within that culture may share certain values, but individuals within the group vary greatly. In addition, what we may think of as a manifestation of the culture may be only an idiosyncrasy of a few individuals.

Questions 2 and 3 specifically ask students to reflect on Native American contributions. They should help to dispel typical stereotypes.

♦ Responding

1. Define a tribe. Lincoln identifies characteristics accepted by all Native American tribes in spite of their diversity. Describe these features.

2. Working individually or in a group, list the contributions of Native Americans to new American immigrants. Share the list with the class and discuss how much of the information is new to you. What are the implications of this history?

3. Review the characteristics and contributions of Native Americans mentioned in the essay. How do these compare with the image currently presented by the media?

4. Lincoln says that "Indians gave names for rivers, mountains, lakes, cities, counties, streets, and over half the states. And they believed in the bonding and animating powers of words — to invoke and actualize the world through a language of experience. Words were not notational labels or signs . . . words were beings in themselves, incantatory, with spirits and bodies." With the class, think of examples of Indian names. How do these names reflect Indian beliefs?

CONNECTING (printed in AMERICAN MOSAIC, p. 633)

Critical Thinking and Writing

All of the sets of connecting questions are designed to point up relationships within chapters as well as across the text. Students should be encouraged to use these questions as topics for formal papers or as models for designing their own questions. They force students to think about broader issues and to acknowledge the similarities of experiences among many diverse groups. In this set of questions, 5, 6, and 7 call for comparisons within the chapter, while 2, 3, 8, and 10 suggest comparisons with other parts of the text.

The research questions in this section ask students to either look back into the history of a Native American leader or to look forward to the future of Native American peoples. Some students may be interested in these topics. All questions could be scaled down to be manageable as paper assignments, but you should also encourage your students to use these questions as a springboard for their own.

CHAPTER 9

CONTEMPORARY VOICES: DIVERSITY AND RENEWAL

Like Chapter 1 this chapter presents the perspectives of several ethnic groups. Here we have included some representative readings that highlight the richness and diversity of the old and new residents who make up American society. We believe these individuals echo many of the concerns that faced both the early immigrants presented in Chapter 1 and those who already resided in this country at that time. The readings in this chapter address the same issues of adjustment, assimilation versus cultural pluralism, pride in heritage, and a general coming to terms with oneself and with multicultural America.

We begin the chapter with readings that present some of the factors that forced people out of their homelands and into America. Then we look at American-born descendants of immigrants and Africans who explore their cultural heritage and what makes it a unique part of the American mosaic.

Beginning: Pre-reading/Writing

Throughout its history, the United States has often been a haven for citizens of other countries who are looking for improved political and economic conditions. Working individually or in a group, speculate about what recent political and economic situations in other countries might make citizens of certain countries choose to emigrate. Discuss why they might come to the United States, the possible problems of immigrating here, and the difficulties they would face once they arrive.

The Beginning exercise asks students to speculate about the recent events in specific countries that might compel people to emigrate. Newspapers are a ready source of material, or students can narrow down the topic and research their school. From admissions they can find out how many foreign students attend their university, where they come from, and so forth. They can interview classmates who are immigrants, foreign exchange students, or children of immigrants. They can contact the foreign student association or club. This is a good way for students to learn that immigration to America, to live or to study, is an ongoing process. In addition, hearing the experiences of classmates who are recent immigrants should enrich their understanding of the readings.

From Immigration and Nationality Act of 1980

We chose the section of the Immigration and Nationality Act of 1980 that deals with asylum procedures because recently many groups have entered the United States under its provisions. In other cases, such as the refugees from El Salvador, asylum has been denied. Students might want to investigate the rationale behind the government's decisions.

Question 1 can begin the post-reading discussion. It aims to get students to attempt to define *refugee* and to appreciate the difficulty in establishing a precise definition. They might first look up the standard definition or create a definition from the context in the reading. Next, they can think of ways to modify that definition. This activity could help focus a follow-up small- or large-group discussion.

The discussion could be followed by a writing assignment based on question 3, which asks students to consider current immigration policy. You can have them choose any recent historical event to define their criteria for asylum . Once students have formulated a policy, they can be divided into groups according to the established criteria. After within-group discussion, each group can select a member to research the question and then participate in an informal debate.

Question 2 will be especially effective if you used the Beginning exercise in class. It gives students the opportunity to internalize the concept of asylum, something most of them have experienced only through the media.

♦ Responding

1. Explain the provisions of the asylum regulations in your own words. If you were writing the law, how would you define *refugee*?

2. Write about the experience of someone you know or have read, studied, or heard about, who has sought asylum in the United States. What circumstances caused this person to leave his or her country? How do you think the circumstances of immigration affected his or her adjustment?

3. What do you think the United States's immigration policy should be? Who should be granted asylum? Choose a recent historical event such as the Tiananmen Square massacre and discuss whether the U.S. should give asylum to participants in that event.

CYNTHIA OZICK
From The Shawl

Knowledge of the events of World War II is needed to understand this reading, so you might review the Holocaust with students. Students probably have seen enough films and television programs to be able to share their knowledge and fill in the historical details. Such information is best presented before the reading to help students understand Rosa and her situation. They might also need to know that Stella is her relative in New York and that Magda, her daughter, died in the camps.

Since one theme of the reading is the attempt to control and change the past through rewriting history, a possible pre-reading activity is to discuss whether rewriting history can actually change people's views. Then question 2 could be used as a follow-up. Alternatively, you can discuss the use of personal writing as therapy. Here you might compare Rosa to the writers of the Gold Mountain poems in Chapter 2 and have students consider question 1.

A post-reading discussion might begin with a ten-minute in-class writing assignment asking students to respond to Dr. Tree as Rosa might (question 3). This could lead to a general discussion of the broader issues brought up in question 4 or to a discussion of Rosa's response to evil.

♦ Responding

1. Rosa calls writing "this capacity, this power to make a history, to tell, to explain. To retrieve, to reprieve! To lie." Explain how her letter to Magda, the child who perished in the Holocaust, does all of these things. Discuss why and to whom Rosa is lying.

2. Write an essay agreeing or disagreeing that events can be rewritten by individuals or by groups to distort history. Support your argument with incidents from the story, your own experience, or your knowledge of current events.

3. Dr. Tree asks Rosa to participate in his study of survivors. Working individually or in a group, discuss why Rosa is so angry at his letter and write the response she might send him. How do you think you would feel in her situation?

4. Discuss the ethical issues involved in studies of victims of tragedies. What benefits might result from such studies? What harmful effects might they produce? How would you balance the knowledge that can be gained with the victim's right to privacy?

TRAN VAN DINH
Truce in Heaven, Peace on Earth

We included this reading because it illustrates the difficulties and dangers that still confront immigrants who are forced to flee their homelands. It also shows the desperation these Vietnamese must have felt to risk this dangerous voyage. As a pre-reading activity, you might review the hardships some of the early immigrants faced during their voyage to America.

If students are particularly interested in the Vietnamese, as a post-reading activity they can divide into groups and have each group research one of the issues in question 1. Then they can share their research with the class. Vietnamese students can serve as resources. If you prefer a more "personal" post-reading activity, you can use question 3 as a follow-up ten-minute in-class writing assignment.

♦ Responding

1. Research the history of the boat people of Vietnam. Working in a group, share the information you have gathered and explore one of the following issues:
    a. the boat people's reasons for leaving Vietnam.
    b. typical conditions aboard the boats
    c. their reception in Thailand
    d. conditions in the refugee camps
    e. their reception in the United States
    Share your conclusions with the class.

2. Explain why the Vietnamese on the boat might have "lowered their heads more in shame and anger than in fear" during the attack by bandits.

3. Imagine having to flee your home and country at a moment's notice. Write an essay or a journal entry discussing your feelings at such a time.

OSCAR HIJUELOS
Visitors, 1965

This reading also details the experiences of political refugees. Hijuelos compares the situation of a family that immigrated in the 1940s with one that immigrates in the 1960s. He reviews the recent history of Cuba and explains why support for Fidel Castro among some Cubans and emigres declined. He also explores a recurring theme in this text: the identity crisis experienced by the bicultural children of immigrants.

You might engage students in a pre-reading discussion by asking them what they know about Cuba and its history. If they know very little, they can anticipate having many of their questions answered by the reading. However, there may be Cuban students in the class who can serve as experts and may be willing to share their own and their families' experiences.

Discussing current immigration and political situations may create controversy in class. For example, students may support one regime or another or may not understand the political situation in a particular country. Most likely you will be reading this section late in the quarter or semester, by which time students should have come to feel that they are part of a community. Community standards of behavior should include listening to everyone and keeping discussions free of personal attacks. As we mentioned earlier, if the classroom situation deteriorates, you can try to get students to write about what happened and then discuss it in class. Understanding why they or someone else acted defensively may help resolve differences.

Question 4 could be used to structure small- or large-group follow-up discussion. Students might discuss whether they sympathize with Mercedes's anger. Alternatively, they may wish to discuss question 1 and explore the political situation in more depth.

If you choose to look at the identity problems encountered by the children of immigrants, you can focus the post-reading discussion on question 3, which replays the recurring conflict experienced in *No-no Boy* (Chapter 5), "Legal Alien" (Chapter 7), and other selections. Hector's feelings about Cuba may also be compared to Marisol's in *The Line of the Sun* (Chapter 4).

♦ Responding

1. Compare Alejo and Mercedes's attitudes toward the Cuban revolution before and after Castro came to power. What would they say to supporters of the revolution, such as their neighbor Señor Lopez?

2. What is Horacio's definition of *culture*? Compare his definition with other meanings.

3. Hector is "sick at heart for being so Americanized, which he 'equates' with being fearful and lonely." Using examples from the reading, explain the ways in which he is Americanized. Compare his feelings about America with his feelings about Cuba. What does Cuba seem to represent to him?

4. Why is Mercedes angry? Compare the situation of the immigrants arriving in 1965 with that of immigrants who arrived twenty years earlier. Why do you think Pedro and his family become prosperous while Alejo and his family remain poor? Using information from the reading and your own knowledge, speculate about each family's reception in the new country.

JOSÉ ALEJANDRO ROMERO
Sumpul

This poem tells of the massacre at Sumpul in 1980, in which six hundred Salvadorans lost their lives. Students will need to read the headnote to understand the historical context of the poem. The political events in El Salvador that took place from May 1979 to May 1980 forced Romero and many other Salvadorans into exile. Twenty-five protesters were massacred in front of the Cathedral of San Salvador (May 8, 1979), twenty-five demonstrators were killed in front of the Venezuelan embassy (May 17, 1980), and Archbishop Oscar Romero was murdered in his church (March 24, 1980). These events were part of a cycle of disappearances and deaths that came to be almost routine.

As a post-reading discussion, you might focus on the effects of these horrors on the survivors and escapees. Students might want to compare their possible reactions, guilt about surviving, fear, anger, hatred, desire for escape, and revenge with Rosa's reactions in Ozick's story.

Even without additional information the poem powerfully evokes the horrors of conflict. Students may want to read it aloud and discuss its dramatic impact. After the reading, students can use question 1 or 2 as the basis for a ten-minute in-class writing assignment.

Question 3 invites students to write about their own experiences. Students might want to discuss the therapeutic effect of writing about a deeply disturbing event. Perhaps this was the author's purpose. A discussion of Romero's purposes in writing a political poem could be the focus of the post-reading discussion, again using comparisons with Rosa and the Gold Mountain poets in Chapter 2.

◆ Responding

1. Explain in your own words what the river has witnessed.

2. How would you describe the speaker in the poem? What is the speaker's situation?

3. The author uses poetry to express his feelings about an important event in his country's history. Write a poem about a place or event that is particularly meaningful to you.

MARK MATHABANE
I Leave South Africa

This reading presents the perspective of a victim of the repressive policies toward blacks in South Africa as he comes in contact with a black separatist in the United

States. A pre-reading discussion might focus on the topic of race and culture. How similar are people of the same racial group? Does race, culture, or both determine identity within a group? Anthropologist Clyde Kluckhohn has conducted considerable research on the importance of culture. He discusses a Caucasian, orphaned in China and raised by Chinese parents, who, despite his fair skin, exhibited the gestures, speech, and customs of the Chinese. Was he Chinese or American (his native land)? Is it heredity or culture that makes you who you are? The point is that in Mathabane's piece, the black separatist assumes a common bond with Mark that Mark does not seem to share.

Separatism as a solution to racism might be the topic of a follow-up discussion. How does separatism differ from apartheid? Questions 1, 2, and 3 can aid in this discussion. If you discuss question 1, you may want to review some of the highlights of the civil rights movement in Chapter 6. As a supplement to question 3, you can encourage students to research Nelson Mandella's 1990 tour of the United States and his speech in Harlem.

♦ Responding

1. Analyze the misunderstandings between Mark and the Black Muslim he meets during the flight to the United States. How do the differences in their backgrounds lead to these misunderstandings?

2. The Black Muslim says, "What good has integration done the black man? We've simply become more dependent on the white devil and forgotten how to do things for ourselves. Also, no matter how integrated we become, white folks won't accept us as equals. So why should we break our backs trying to mix with them, heh?" Agree or disagree with this statement, supporting your argument with evidence from this reading and your own knowledge and experience.

3. Working individually or in a group, list the differences in life situations, freedom, and opportunity for blacks in South Africa and blacks in America.

JESSICA HAGEDORN
Luna Moth

This reading reflects the problems of many new immigrants who find they really do not fit into their new surroundings but have changed enough to be alienated from their old ones. Students might want to compare this narrator with Hanneh Brineh in "The Fat of the Land" (Chapter 1), Hector in "Visitors, 1965" (Chapter 9), or Marisol in the excerpt from *The Line of the Sun* (Chapter 4) (see question 4).

A pre-reading discussion could begin with the question of whether one can go home again. Students might bring up problems they may have encountered in going home during college breaks: How does the old neighborhood seem? Can they still fit in? How do they feel in their new environment? A post-reading discussion can center around question 2. Question 3 may also provide a good follow-up to this approach and give students the opportunity to write personal responses.

Another possibility is to ask students to compare the speaker's disillusionment with America with the reactions of other immigrants. Students should consider the effects of immigration and the situation in the new country on immigrants' adjustment.

♦ Responding

1. Speculate on the reasons for the narrator's initial enthusiasm about going to live in America and what might have made her unhappy once she was living there. Do you think the family she left behind or the culture she encounters is responsible?

2. When the speaker returns to Manila for a visit, her father warns her against visiting her old house, saying, "You'll be disappointed. Memories are always better." In what ways are her memories different from reality? Write an essay agreeing or disagreeing with her father's opinion. Support your argument with examples from the reading or from your own experience.

3. The narrator conveys some of her pain when she says, "I am anxious and restless, at home only in airports." She seems to belong nowhere. Write a journal entry about a time when you or someone you know felt uncomfortable or out of place in a new situation.

4. Compare the narrator's feelings of dislocation and disorientation with the feelings of any of the other immigrants you have read about in this text.

MIKE ROSE
From Lives on the Boundary

Since Rose describes his early environment in this chapter from his book, students might begin by thinking about the effects of environment on achievement: Do you think where you grew up and the neighborhood you lived in affected your chances for future academic or economic success? In what way is adversity an incentive? In what way is it a disincentive?

After reading, you might have students review Rose's accomplishments, which are listed in the headnote, and discuss question 4. For more personal responses, you can use question 2. Students interested in a career in education or concerned about current problems in education can be encouraged to read *Lives on the Boundary*.

♦ Responding

1. Compare Rose's neighborhood with the place where you grew up. In your description, include the opportunities and role models available to him and to you.

2. Rose characterizes his parents as "two more poor settlers trying to make a go of it in the City of the Angels." Compare the myth of California with the realities encountered by Rose's parents.

3. Rose says, "What finally affected me was subtler, but more persuasive: I cannot recall a young person who was crazy in love or lost in work or one old person who was passionate about a cause or an idea. . . . The people I grew up with were retired from jobs that rub away the heart or were working hard at jobs to keep their lives from caving in . . . junkies, alcoholics, and mean kids walking along Vermont [Avenue] looking to throw a punch. I developed a picture of human existence that rendered it short and brutish or sad and aimless. . . ." What are the possible psychological and social effects on a child of growing up in such a neighborhood? This kind of environment can severely limit a young person's opportunities for academic and economic success, yet, in spite of his background, Rose achieved academic success. What factors do you think counter the effects of environment?

ALICE WALKER
Everyday Use

Although this story has been anthologized frequently, we included it because it so clearly states the themes of this text: exploring culture and heritage and determining their roles in an individual's life. The attitudes of the women in this story toward the past differ, but in the end all wish to preserve it. For Dee, the daughter, the family relics are no longer a stigma but things to be treasured. Although we may disagree with Dee's attitude, certainly it is healthier for her to be proud of her past than to want to forget it. At the same time, Dee represents a person who takes up culture as a fad and may well drop it just as quickly when it is no longer fashionable.

This story also provides an opportunity for students to discuss some important aspect of their cultural heritage. You might ask them to define *heritage* and

discuss their definitions. After reading this piece, any of the questions can be used
to focus post-reading large- or small-group discussions.

Question 3 can be used directly following the reading. By rewriting the story
from another point of view, students will have to articulate the reasons for a
character's actions that Walker only implies. Discussion could follow a reading of
some of the other versions. This could lead to a more in-depth approach to one of
the other Responding questions.

♦ Responding

1. The mother believes that Dee is ashamed of her house, saying, "No doubt when
   Dee sees it she will want to tear it down." Yet when Dee arrives she
   immediately wants to photograph it. What explains her changed attitude to
   the house and its contents?

2. Dee accuses her mother of not understanding their heritage. Heritage means
   something very different to these women. Compare their definitions. Then,
   using those definitions, argue that either Maggie or Dee should have the quilt.

3. The story is told from the point of view of the mother. Retell it from the point of
   view of one of the other characters.

4. Objects from the past can often be meaningful reminders of tradition and
   family. What important objects in the story might represent the family's
   experience as blacks in America? Describe an object owned by your family that
   represents an important event in your family's history and in your cultural
   heritage.

DAVID MURA
Strangers in the Village

This final reading sums up our reasons for compiling this collection. Many racial
groups have gone through school with exposure to only white and European
history and literature. Mura makes an eloquent argument for a multicultural
curriculum. Now that this issue currently is being debated at colleges across the
country, your students, having completed a course using this text, might want to
join in the debate. With the exposure to minority authors that they received in this
course and to mainstream authors throughout their school careers, students can
use their reactions to formulate their own "ideal" curriculum. Question 2 could set
up a debate between advocates of a return to the "'classics" and supporters of a
cross-cultural curriculum for freshman English courses, as has been done at
Stanford University. Students might want to pursue this issue with administrators
of the school, of affirmative action programs, and so forth, to learn about the

situation on their campus. Even a look at the readings list for courses would be revealing.

Some questions for discussion include the following:

1. Who should take ethnic literature or history courses? Should these courses be designed for members of a particular ethnic group? Should students who enroll in a freshman English class be required to read minority group writers?
2. If classes focus on minority issues and are attended primarily by members of the particular groups, might they "ghettoize" minorities on campus?
3. Is a multicultural society a desirable goal, or would it threaten our American identity and values?

Hopefully, a course such as this not only would increase students' interest in and knowledge about other cultures but enhance their interest in their own cultures. Question 4 provides an opportunity to focus on those interests.

Although this selection appears at the end of the text, the issues raised here could be discussed at the beginning of the course. Some students may resent spending a course on immigrant and ethnic experiences. Airing these concerns early is one way to explain the purposes of the course and to allow students to vent their reluctance and remove any obstacles to learning.

♦ Responding

1. In this reading, Barbra represents all whites. Explain what Mura wants Barbra to do to help redress the wrongs in our society. What practical steps do you think she can take? How will her actions further understanding between the races?

2. Discuss Mura's response to critics who call for "a return to the classics and a notion of a core-cultural tradition" and who "bemoan . . . the multicultural movements which, in the name of 'tolerance,' have supposedly left our culture in a shambles."

3. Mura says "the images I grew up with in the media were all white," and "the books I read in school — from Dick and Jane onwards — were about whites and later, about European civilization." What would his reaction to a text such as this one probably be? Would he want all students or only members of ethnic minorities to read such a text? Discuss the effects on both whites and members of other groups of learning about cultures other than European.

4. Working in a group, discuss what Mura means when he says, ". . . this is not to say I now regret what I know but I do regret what I don't know." List things about your own background and culture that you would like to know more about. Share your list with the class.

CONNECTING (printed in AMERICAN MOSAIC, p. 708)

Critical Thinking and Writing

Most of the questions in this section ask students to draw comparisons or cite examples from other parts of the text. At this point in the semester or quarter, students should have read enough of the other readings to be able to find examples easily. Questions 1, 4, and 10 suggest comparisons between readings within the chapter. Questions 2, 3, 6, 8, 9, and 11 ask students to compare specific issues raised in this chapter with suggested selections from other chapters. Questions 4, 5, 7, and 12 ask students to discuss broad issues that recur through the readings.

The research topics require outside information. They primarily focus on issues of public policy.

For general suggestions about ways to use the questions see the connecting section in Chapter 1 of this manual.

PART THREE

THEMATIC TABLE OF CONTENTS

We chose to organize the readings in this text by historical theme because we believe that understanding the context enhances students' appreciation of both the works and the cultures represented. That is not to say, however, that these readings should be restricted to the periods in which they were written. In fact, throughout the text and this manual we have attempted to point up significant themes that recur across cultures and across time.

If you prefer to organize your class thematically, you may find the following thematic table of contents helpful. Needless to say, not every reading has been assigned to a category, and some have been included in several categories. You also might have ideas that you'd like to pursue that haven't been considered here. Please bear in mind that this list is meant only to suggest options, not to restrict interpretation.

AMERICAN DREAM

COLÓN *Kipling and I*
THE GOLD MOUNTAIN POEMS *Immigration Blues*
KELLY *A Soul Above Buttons*
KINGSTON *The Grandfather of the Sierra Nevada Mountains*
LOWE *Father Cures a Presidential Fever*
PANUNZIO *In the American Storm*
RIVERA, E. *Ropes of Passage*
ROSE from *Lives on the Boundary*
YAMAMOTO *Las Vegas Charley*
YEZIERSKA *The Fat of the Land*

ARRIVING IN AMERICA

COLÓN *Stowaway*
FAR *In the Land of the Free*
HAGEDORN *Luna Moth*
HIJUELOS *Visitors, 1965*
KINGSTON *The Grandfather of the Sierra Nevada Mountains*
MATHABANE *I Leave South Africa*

ROSE   from *Lives on the Boundary*
THOMAS   *Puerto Rican Paradise*
WALKER   *Everyday Use*
YEZIERSKA   *The Fat of the Land*

LOOKING TO THE HOMELAND

ALLEN   *Where I Come from Is Like This*
COFER   from *The Line of the Sun*
HAGEDORN   *Luna Moth*
HIJUELOS   *Visitors, 1965*
MATHABANE   *I Leave South Africa*
MOHR   *A Thanksgiving Celebration*
OKADA   from *No-no Boy*
ROMERO   *Sumpul*
THOMAS   *Puerto Rican Paradise*
WALKER   *Everyday Use*

TRADITIONS

ALLEN   *Where I Come from Is Like This*
COFER   from *The Line of the Sun*
ERDRICH   from *Love Medicine*
LOWE   *Father Cures a Presidential Fever*
MOHR   *A Thanksgiving Celebration*
MOMADAY   *January 26*
RIVERA, T.   *Christmas Eve/La Noche Buena*
VEGA   *The customs and traditions of the* tabaqueros *and what it was like to work in a cigar factory in New York City*
WALKER   *Everyday Use*
WELCH   *Plea to Those Who Matter*
WELCH   *Riding the Earthboy 40*
YEZIERSKA   *The Fat of the Land*

WOMEN

ALLEN   *Where I Come from Is Like This*
CASTILLO   *Milagros*
CISNEROS   *Woman Hollering Creek*
ERDRICH   from *Love Medicine*
FAR   *In the Land of the Free*
HURSTON   *Sweat*
MIRIKITANI   *Desert Flowers*
MOHR   *A Thanksgiving Celebration*
MORA   *Illegal Alien*

PART FOUR

SUGGESTED FILMS

In assembling this list of films, we chose only those productions that we felt would complement the historical information and general themes in the text. As a result, we were able to locate more films for some chapters than others. Remember, however, that new films are constantly being released and an occasional glance through film source guides can keep you informed of new materials. We found the following guides to be informative, and you may wish to refer to them for additional information: *Educational Film and Video Locator*, R. R. Bowker; *Films and Video for History and Politics*, Penn State Audio-Visual Services; *Native Americans on Film and Video*, Museum of the American Indian/Heye Foundation; and *The Video Source Book*, Gale Research Inc.

At the end of each entry, we have listed the distributor. An index of these distributors and their addresses is given at the end of the film suggestion list.

CHAPTER 1

America: 9 — The Huddled Masses

Alistair Cooke describes immigration to the United States at the end of the 19th century.

52 min./color
DIST: AMB

The Immigrant Experience: The Long, Long Journey

Focuses on the problems and dreams of newly landed immigrants in America by dramatizing the struggle of a twelve-year-old Polish immigrant and his family to survive after their arrival in 1907.

28 min./color
DIST: LCA

A Storm of Strangers: Jewish-Americans

Photographs of New York's Lower East Side are used to illustrate the story of Jewish immigration to America around the year 1910.

27 min./b&w.
DIST: FI

CHAPTER 2

The Chinese-Americans: The Early Immigrants

This film presents the history and contributions of the first Chinese who immigrated to America.

20 min./color
DIST: HFC

The Golden Mountain on Mott Street

Examines the problems encountered by Chinese immigrants to the United States.

38 min./color
DIST: WCBS

A Storm of Strangers: Jung Sai, Chinese-American

A Chinese American journalist traces her heritage by interviewing Chinese of all ages about the early immigrant experience, including building the transcontinental railway, working in the mines, and establishing Chinatowns.

29 min./color
DIST: FI

CHAPTER 3

Black Paths of Leadership: Washington, DuBois, and Garvey

Traces the lives and philosophies of three spokesmen for African Americans in the early 20th century, Booker T. Washington, W. E. B. DuBois, and Marcus Garvey.

27 min./color
DIST: CHUH

From These Roots

This film on the 1920s Harlem Renaissance features the work of Cab Calloway, Paul Robeson, Ethel Waters, Duke Ellington, Langston Hughes, and Claude MacKay.

28 min./b&w
DIST: YOURWV

I Remember Harlem: Part 1 — The Early Years, 1600–1930

The first of a three part series, this film traces the development of Harlem including the 369th Infantry's return home after World War I, the black nationalist Marcus Garvey movement, and the Harlem Renaissance of the 1920s.

58 min./color
DIST: FFHS

CHAPTER 4

An Island in America

This program examines the cultural, social, and economic life of Puerto Ricans in the United States.

28 min./color
DIST: ADLBB

Puerto Rico: Americans on the Move

This film explores some of the causes and effects of the migration of Puerto Ricans to New York City and other metropolitan centers.

55 min./b&w
DIST: CBS TV; MCGH

Puerto Rico: Migration

This film examines the migration of Puerto Ricans to the United States mainland and the problems they face in their new homes. Compares Puerto Rican migration with the waves of Europeans who came to America during the late 19th and early 20th centuries.

9 min./color
DIST: STERLED

CHAPTER 5

Family Gathering

Japanese filmmaker, Lisa Yasui, uses interviews, home movies, historical footage, and stills to present the experiences of her people in the United States. Special focus is given to the repercussions of her grandfather's internment.

30 min.
DIST: NEWDAY

Guilty by Reason of Race

This film focuses on the events that followed the issue of the Japanese Internment Order. Interviews individuals who went through the experience, some of whom subsequently left the United States and others who remained.

52 min./color
DIST: FI

Invisible Citizens — Japanese Americans

How six Japanese Americans' lives were affected by their internment in concentration camps during World War II.

58 min./color
DIST: Downtown Community TV Center

CHAPTER 6

Civil Rights Movement: The North

Looks at job discrimination, attempted housing integration, and the tense atmosphere of race relations in northern U.S. cities.

22 min./b&w
DIST: FI

Civil Rights Movement: The South

Surveys civil rights movements in areas of education, public accommodations, and voting rights.

28 min./b&w
DIST: FI

Daughters of the Black Revolution

Daughters of slain civil rights leaders Martin Luther King, Jr., Medgar Evers, and Malcolm X talk with Phil Donahue.

28 min./color
DIST: FFHS

Do the Right Thing

Portrays the racial tensions surrounding a white-owned pizzeria in the Bed-Stuyvesant section of Brooklyn on the hottest day of the summer, and the violence that eventually erupts.

95 min./color
DIST: MCA Home Video

El-Hajj Malik El-Shabazz: Malcolm X

Profiles the life of Malcolm X, focusing on the ideas and personal qualities that made him an important leader of the civil rights movement in America in the 1960s.

55 min./b&w
DIST: CRMP

Eyes on the Prize

A comprehensive six-part series on the history of the American Civil Rights Movement from World War II to the present.

60 min./color
DIST: PBS Video

Now Is the Time

Recounts the history of African Americans through film clips and dramatic readings, contrasting myths about the "good Negro" of the old minstrel shows with scenes of police beatings and sit-ins in the 1960s.

36 min./b&w
DIST: CARSL

CHAPTER 7

Harvest of Shame

A documentary study, narrated by Edward R. Murrow, of the degradation and exploitation of millions of migrant workers in the United States.

53 min./b&w
DIST: CRM

Mexican Americans: An Historic Profile

This program looks at the history of the Mexican American from the Spanish Conquistadores to the present.

29 min./b&w
DIST: ADLBB

The Migrants, 1980

Examines the conditions under which itinerant farm workers lived and worked in 1980, and looks at what,if anything, changed for these workers in the twenty years since *Harvest of Shame* (see above) was broadcast.

50 min./color
DIST: FI

One River, One Country: The U.S.-Mexico Border

Correspondent Bill Moyers investigates the "third country" that has emerged along the Rio Grande River, where inhabitants share family and economic ties but feel isolated from the cultures of their native lands, Mexico and the United States.

47 min./color
DIST: CARSL

Raymund Paredes on Chicano Literature

Raymund Paredes, a leading specialist in Chicano cultural studies, discusses the roots and current directions of Chicano literature.

30 min./color
DIST: KPBS

CHAPTER 8

Ancient Spirit, Living Word: The Oral Tradition

This film examines Native American story telling.

58 min./color
DIST: Native American Public Broadcasting Consortium

The Forgotten American

The story of the economic, social, and spiritual plight of American Indians.

25 min./color
DIST: CARSL

Images of Indians

A five part series that traces the stereotypical Hollywood treatment of Indians through the years.

30 min./color
DIST: UINDIANS; Video Tech

Indian Self-Rule: A Problem of History

Presents a historical outline of federal Indian policy, focusing on the question of tribal sovereignty.

58 min./color
DIST: DER

Voices of Native Americans

By documenting two Native American conferences, this film looks at different approaches Native American leaders are taking to solve current problems.

58 min./color
DIST: TWNEWS

CHAPTER 9

Against Wind and Tide: A Cuban Odyssey

This film focuses on the Cuban refugees who came during the Mariel boatlift in 1980 to show the inconsistencies in American immigration policy.

55 min./color
DIST: FML

The Constitution: That Delicate Balance 11 — Immigration Reform

Examines the criteria for admitting foreigners into the United States, legal aliens' rights to social services, employers' responsibilities in hiring undocumented persons, and the extent to which illegal aliens have rights.

56 min./color
DIST: INTELL

The Phans of Jersey City

Documentary portrait of a twenty-member Vietnamese refugee family living in the United States showing how the different family members survive.

49 min./color
DIST: FI

Wanting It All — Immigrant's Dream

Looks at a cross-section of immigrants in discussing the rise of legal and illegal immigration in the United States.

22 min./color
DIST: NBC; CARSL

PRODUCER/DISTRIBUTOR LIST

ADLBB
Anti-Defamation League of B'nai B'rith
823 United Nations Plaza
New York, NY 10017

AMB
Ambrose Video Publishing, Inc.
381 Park Ave. South, Suite 1601
New York, NY 10016

CARSL
Carousel Film and Video
260 Fifth Ave.
New York, NY 10001

CBS
Columbia Broadcasting System
383 Madison Ave.
New York, NY 10017

CHUH
Churchill Films
12210 Nebraska Ave.
Los Angeles, CA 90025

CRM
See MCGH

DER
Documentary Educational Resources
5 Bridge St.
Watertown, MA 02172

Downtown Community TV Center
87 Lafayette St.
New York, NY 10013

FFHS
Films for the Humanities, Inc.
P.O. Box 2053
Princeton, NJ 08540

FI
Films, Inc., Public Media, Inc.
5547 Ravenswood Ave.
Chicago, IL 60640

FML
Filmakers Library, Inc.
124 E. 40th St., Suite 901
New York, NY 10016

HFC
Handel Film Corporation
8730 Sunset Blvd.
Los Angeles, CA 90069

INTELL
Intellimation, Inc.
2040 Alameda Padre Serra
P.O. Box 4069
Santa Barbara, CA 93140

KPBS
San Diego State University
San Diego, CA 92182

LCA
Learning Corporation of America
Dist. by: Simon and Schuster Communications
108 Wilmot Road
Deerfield, IL 60015

MCA
MCA Home Video
70 Universal City Plaza
Universal City, CA 91608

MCGH
CRM Films
2233 Faraday Ave.
Carlsbad, CA 92008

NAPBC
P.O. Box 83111
Lincoln, NE 68501

NBC
National Broadcasting Company
30 Rockefeller Plaza
New York, NY 10020

NEWDAY
New Day Films
853 Broadway, Suite 1210
New York, NY 10003

PBS
PBS Video
1320 Braddock Place
Alexandria, VA 22314

STERLED
Sterling Educational Films, Inc.
241 E. 34 St.
New York, NY 10016

TWNEWS
Third World Newsreel
160 Fifth Ave., Room 911
New York, NY 10010

UINDIANS
United Indians Of All Tribes Foundation
Administrative Office
Discovery Park
Seattle, WA 98104

Video Tech
19346 3rd Ave., NW
Seattle, WA 98177

WCBS
WCBS-TV
524 W. 57 St.
New York, NY 10019

YOURWV
Your World Video, Inc.
80 8th Ave.
Suite 1701
New York, NY 10011